Improving Teacher Morale and Motivation

Improving Teacher Morale and Motivation discusses a key issue for school leaders: motivating teachers to improve learning for students. Immense and unprecedented changes in education—primarily with the pandemic and "great resignation"—have affected all areas of teaching and learning, including teacher morale and motivation. This engaging book takes an in-depth focus on student learning as it relates to teacher motivation, providing specific examples of how to motivate teachers during challenging times. Specific tools, templates, and strategies are incorporated throughout the book to help leaders understand and act on issues of intrinsic and extrinsic motivation, collaboration and trust, growth mindset, effective feedback, and more. Further, this text incorporates a broader look at how school leaders can shape their school and make it a place where teachers want to work, where they are committed to the success of students, and where they see themselves remaining well into the future. This timely book is appropriate for all school leaders, including teacher-leaders and district leaders.

Ronald Williamson is Professor Emeritus of educational leadership at Eastern Michigan University, USA. He is a former principal, central office administrator, and executive director of the National Middle School Association (now AMLE).

Barbara R. Blackburn, a "Top 30 Global Guru in Education," is the best-selling author of over 30 books and is a sought-after national and international consultant. She was an award-winning professor at Winthrop University and has taught early childhood, elementary, middle, and high school students.

Other Eye On Education Books Available from Routledge
(www.routledge.com/eyeoneducation)

Leading School Culture through Teacher Voice and Agency
Sally J. Zepeda, Philip D. Lanoue, David R. Shafer, Grant M. Rivera

Becoming an International School Educator: Stories, Tips, and Insights from Teachers and Leaders
Edited by Dana Specker Watts and Jayson W. Richardson

The Confident School Leader: 7 Keys to Influence and Implement Change
Kara Knight

Rigor in Your Classroom: A Toolkit for Teachers
Barbara R. Blackburn

Rigor for Students with Special Needs
Barbara R. Blackburn, Bradley Steven Witzel

Rigor in the Remote Learning Classroom: Instructional Tips and Strategies
Barbara R. Blackburn

7 Strategies for Improving Your School
Ronald Williamson and Barbara R. Blackburn

Money for Good Grades and Other Myths About Motivating Kids: Strategies for Parents and Teachers
Barbara R. Blackburn

Leadership for Remote Learning: Strategies for Success
Ronald Williamson and Barbara R. Blackburn

Advocacy from A to Z
Robert Blackburn, Barbara R. Blackburn, and Ronald Williamson

Improving Teacher Morale and Motivation

Leadership Strategies that Build Student Success

Ronald Williamson and Barbara R. Blackburn

Routledge
Taylor & Francis Group
NEW YORK AND LONDON

Designed cover image: © Getty Images

First published 2024
by Routledge
605 Third Avenue, New York, NY 10158

and by Routledge
4 Park Square, Milton Park, Abingdon, Oxon, OX14 4RN

Routledge is an imprint of the Taylor & Francis Group, an informa business

© 2024 Ronald Williamson and Barbara R. Blackburn

The right of Ronald Williamson and Barbara R. Blackburn to be identified as authors of this work has been asserted in accordance with sections 77 and 78 of the Copyright, Designs and Patents Act 1988.

All rights reserved. The purchase of this copyright material confers the right on the purchasing institution to photocopy or download pages which bear a copyright line at the bottom of the page. No other parts of this book may be reprinted or reproduced or utilised in any form or by any electronic, mechanical, or other means, now known or hereafter invented, including photocopying and recording, or in any information storage or retrieval system, without permission in writing from the publishers.

Trademark notice: Product or corporate names may be trademarks or registered trademarks, and are used only for identification and explanation without intent to infringe.

Library of Congress Cataloging-in-Publication Data
Names: Williamson, Ronald D., author. | Blackburn, Barbara R., 1961– author.
Title: Improving teacher morale and motivation : leadership strategies that build student success / Ronald Williamson and Barbara R. Blackburn.
Description: New York : Routledge, 2024. | Includes bibliographical references.
Identifiers: LCCN 2023011091 | ISBN 9781032315133 (hbk) | ISBN 9781032315959 (pbk) | ISBN 9781003310471 (ebk)
Subjects: LCSH: Teacher morale—United States. | Teachers—Job satisfaction. | Motivation in education. | School personnel management. | Teachers—In-service training.
Classification: LCC LB2833.2 .W5 2024 | DDC 371.1001/9—dc23/eng/20230510
LC record available at https://lccn.loc.gov/2023011091

ISBN: 978-1-032-31513-3 (hbk)
ISBN: 978-1-032-31595-9 (pbk)
ISBN: 978-1-003-31047-1 (ebk)

DOI: 10.4324/9781003310471

Typeset in Palatino
by Apex CoVantage, LLC

Access the Support Material: www.routledge.com/9781032315959

I've had an opportunity to work with teachers and school leaders from urban, suburban, and rural communities. You amaze me with your creativity, your perseverance, and most of all, your dedication to your students and your communities. I learn so much from all of you. Thank you for your continued commitment to a quality education for each of your students.
—Ronald Williamson

I dedicate this book to my husband, whose leadership motivated and inspired his employees to do their best.
—Barbara R. Blackburn

Contents

Meet the Authors ix
Preface xi
Acknowledgments xv
Support Materials xvii

1 **Extrinsic and Intrinsic Motivation** 1

2 **Growth Mindset and Resilience** 13

3 **A School's Reputation: The Intersection Between Climate and Culture** 27

4 **SCT Effective Support: Listen, Then Build a System** 39

5 **Hiring and Retaining Faculty** 53

6 **What's Trust Got to Do with It?** 69

7 **Empowerment and Ownership** 79

8 **Building Morale through Modeling** 101

9 **Challenges and Concerns** 117

   References 127

Meet the Authors

Ronald Williamson is a professor emeritus of educational leadership at Eastern Michigan University. He previously taught at the University of North Carolina at Greensboro and was a public school administrator in Michigan. Ron has also served as the executive director of the National Middle School Association (now AMLE) and President of the National Forum to Accelerate Middle Grades Reform. Ron is the author of numerous articles, chapters, and books on leadership and effective leadership practices. He's worked with schools across the country, including several large urban districts, as a leadership coach funded by the Edna McConnell Clark Foundation and the Galef Institute of Los Angeles, with suburban districts on a variety of school reform issues and with rural Oregon districts on issues of college access for underrepresented groups.

Barbara R. Blackburn, PhD, one of the "Top 30 Global Gurus in Education," has dedicated her life to raising the level of rigor and motivation for professional educators and students alike. What differentiates Barbara's over 30 books are her easily executable concrete examples based on decades of experience as a teacher, professor, and consultant. Barbara has taught early childhood, elementary, middle, and high school students and has served as an educational consultant for three publishing companies. She holds a master's degree in school administration and was certified as a teacher and a school principal in North Carolina. She received her doctorate in curriculum and teaching from the University of North Carolina at Greensboro. In 2006, she received the award for Outstanding Junior Professor at Winthrop University. She left her position at the University of North Carolina at Charlotte to write and speak full-time. She speaks remotely and in person at state, national, and international conferences, as well as regularly presenting workshops for teachers and administrators in elementary, middle, and high schools. Both her on-site and virtual presentations and workshops are lively and engaging and filled with practical information. For more information, or to schedule professional development, please contact her at her website: www.barbarablackburnonline.com.

Preface

Public education has changed dramatically in recent years. These changes have affected all areas of teaching and learning, but they also heavily impacted teacher morale and motivation. The arrival of the pandemic changed things in an instant. Virtually every school in America closed and shifted to some variation of online learning. Overnight, teachers skilled at face-to-face teaching were expected to move instruction online, often with little training. When schools returned to face-to-face learning, some were even responsible for teaching both remote students as well as those in their classrooms.

There was greater urgency about public health issues and assuring the safety of both students and staff. Requirements for masks or social distancing were often mandates from health authorities. Those requirements shifted week to week, and school personnel were often not involved in shaping them but were responsible for implementation.

At the same time, politicians in many states began to substitute their thinking about curriculum and instruction for those of educators. Mandates were issued by executive order, or changes in state law, to prohibit discussion of some "hot button" social issues.

The Dilemma for Schools

Teachers and other school personnel often bore the brunt of parent and community complaints over how schools responded to these issues. It's a tough time to be a teacher. They're often burned out, demoralized, and considering leaving the profession. And many of the decisions shaping their decision are made by people who don't work in schools. Teachers, and other school personnel, have little control over their own work lives.

The demands placed on educators, and the increasingly political environment shaping school policy, have led many teachers to reconsider teaching as an occupation (Fox, 2021; Kamenetz, 2022). This occurred at the same time that enrollment in colleges of education was declining and fewer teacher candidates were graduating from college (Goldberg, 2021). Nationwide, a shortage of teachers in many key content areas has forced school administrators to struggle to staff schools.

While grappling with these issues, schools also face a generational change as experienced teachers from the "baby boom" generation retire. Younger hires from "Generation Z" hold starkly different views about the workplace, about leadership, and about work–life balance. One significant characteristic of Generation Z is their comfort changing occupations if they are not satisfied or don't find the workplace reflects their norms and values (Fuscaldo, 2021). That willingness to move to a new position, often called the "great resignation," has the potential to provide even greater instability for schools.

What Does a Leader Do?

This changing dynamic means school leaders must adopt a more proactive approach to leading their schools. It's not sufficient to lead the same way, or in the same style, as you've done before.

One surprising characteristic of younger employees is their acknowledgment that they often choose where to work based on the leader, their espoused values, and the values that guide their work, as well as their leadership style.

That's a very powerful idea. Teachers choose to work in schools where they see a congruence between their values and beliefs and those of the leader. And if that congruence is absent, they're willing to transfer to another school or leave the profession to work in another related field.

Morale and Motivation

So this book is not just another book about motivation discussing both intrinsic and extrinsic motivation and other factors. It will incorporate a broader look at how school leaders shape their school and make it a place where teachers want to work, where they are committed to the success of students and where they see themselves remaining well into the future.

That will require leaders to look closely at their own leadership style and the values that shape that style. It also means that leaders must recognize the complex interaction between leadership and a school's culture and climate. We'll explore how to build respectful, collaborative relationships built on a foundation of trust.

We will delve into motivation, but we will also look at a whole set of other issues that contribute to nurturing and sustaining teacher morale. Those efforts are often grounded in the regularities of school life, from the way to recruit teachers, welcome them to the staff, provide opportunities for involvement and professional growth, and build ownership in the success of everyone, but most importantly students.

Often, those routines are just part of the "way we do things" in schools. But we suggest that conditions require leaders to re-examine even the most fundamental routines and norms so that their schools are successful in this new environment.

Overview of Chapters

In Chapter 1, we'll discuss extrinsic and intrinsic motivation, with an emphasis on the characteristics of each. Chapter 2 addresses growth mindset and resilience, two key aspects that allow teachers to continue to move forward in the face of adversity and challenge. We'll look at how a school's reputation impacts motivation, as well as how culture and climate are a part of reputation in Chapter 3. Chapter 4 explores the hiring and retention factors related to motivation and morale. In Chapter 5, we'll look at the critical role trust plays in schools, then we'll turn our attention to ownership and empowerment in Chapter 6. Chapter 7 is focused on modeling—how does what we do and say impact our teachers? Finally, we'll wrap up the book in Chapter 9 with an examination of issues leaders face related to motivation and morale.

Features

Throughout the book, you'll find opportunities to both reflect on your own practice and take action. "Reflection Point," "Take Action," and "Assess Yourself" are the key features to look for. Additionally, starting in Chapter 3, you'll see the "Motivation Connection" at the start of the chapter. This will help you connect the content of the chapter directly with key aspects of motivation.

Final Thoughts

We hope you will use this information to reframe the concepts of morale and motivation through the lens of leadership and school change. The chapters do not have to be read in order; pick and choose the topics that are most pertinent to you. If you have any questions or would like to provide feedback, please contact us through Barbara's website at www.barbarablackburnonline.com.

Acknowledgments

- Ron's wife, Marsha, for her love and support as he undertook yet another writing project.
- Ron's daughter and daughter-in-law, both elementary school teachers, as well as his son-in-law, an elementary school principal, for the opportunity to learn about the "real" world of schools, and to his grandchildren, who constantly provide inspiration and from whom he learned what works to motivate students.
- Ron's former colleagues in the Department of Leadership and Counseling at Eastern Michigan University, who always provided inspiration, encouragement, and support.
- Barbara's best friend, Abbigail Armstrong, whose ongoing encouragement keeps her going.
- Barbara's mom, who reminds her, "You always have two choices: you can be miserable, or you can make the best of the situation."
- John Maloney for a fabulous cover design.
- Kate Fornadel of Apex CoVantage for production and design.
- Heather Jarrow, for her support as our editor.
- Thank you to the hundreds of school leaders we've worked with in every part of the world. Your dedication to your students and teachers inspires us and all those around you.

Support Materials

These resources can be downloaded, printed, used to copy/paste text, and/or manipulated to suit your individualized use. You can access the downloads by visiting this book's product page on our website: www.routledge.com/9781032315959 (then follow the links indicating related resources, which you can then download directly to your computer).

- Chapter 1: Maslow's Needs
- Chapter 2: Lesson Study Protocol, Lesson Study Observation
- Chapter 3: Assess Yourself
- Chapter 4: Assess Yourself (Listening)
- Chapter 5: Discussion Prompts
- Chapter 6: Leadership Behaviors That Build Trust
- Chapter 7: Assess Yourself
- Chapter 9: Assess Yourself

1
Extrinsic and Intrinsic Motivation

> Motivation Connection:
> Motivation can be extrinsic or intrinsic. Intrinsic motivation is made up of value, meaning relevance, autonomy, relationships, and success.

Do you have faculty or staff who are not motivated? The truth is, all adults are motivated, just not necessarily by their work. So let us rephrase our question. Do you work with adults who are not motivated? Of course you do. And you also work with many who are very motivated.

What is the difference between a motivated and unmotivated adult? See if the following characteristics reflect your adults.

Motivated Adults	*Unmotivated Adults*
Engaged Focused on growth Interacts with others Offers ideas Open to new ideas and activities	Disengaged Lack of interest Isolated Often negative Prefers status quo

Does that look familiar? Of course, the real issue is not identifying an adult's motivation—it's understanding and dealing with it.

DOI: 10.4324/9781003310471-1

Reflection Point: Think about your faculty. Who is motivated? Who isn't?

Many things impact motivation, especially low motivation. These can be placed into three categories: personal factors, work influences, and outside issues (see figure below).

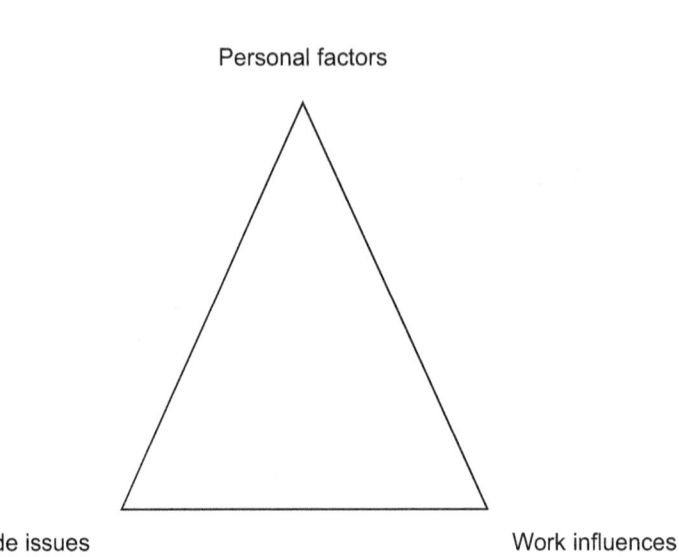

Personal Factors

Adults may have emotional or physical problems that impact their work and their motivation. It may be their own problem or that of a family member or someone they know. The brother of one of Barbara's teachers was tragically killed in a car accident and experienced severe nightmares, anxiety, and depression. Despite his best efforts, his motivation—and his teaching—suffered. Adults may also have low self-efficacy. This may be due to their own struggles in school or college, vicarious experiences, or negative reinforcement from others. Finally, adults may have little interest in their work. Some people feel trapped in their career choice and can't act to make a change.

Work-Based Factors

Besides personal factors, there may be school- or classroom-based factors that impact motivation. Sometimes a work assignment doesn't match one's interests, or a teacher may feel his or her strengths are underutilized.

We mentioned lack of interest as a personal factor, but it is related to work. The majority of Barbara's teaching was in grades 7 and 8. Her major interest was in the primary grades. For her, she found a passion for older students, but if she had not, this may have been problematic.

A final demotivating work-based factor is the lack of perceived power or control. Too often, teachers feel powerless, impacted by curricular or instruction dictates and/or state and local policy. They do not feel like they have any power, which leads to a lack of motivation.

Decisions Often Made for Teachers

Curriculum
Testing
Assessments
Textbooks and other resources
Professional development
Schedules

Outside Factors

Reflection Point: Think about your faculty. What are some of the factors that influence them?

The final influencers on adult motivation are outside ones, such as family issues, attitudes of peers and friends, the reputation of the school and/or district, and the local, state, and national perception of teachers. Each of these may impact a teacher's motivation.

Maslow's Hierarchy of Needs

Before we finish our discussion of overall motivational characteristics, there is another framework to consider. Maslow (1968) identified a hierarchy of needs that people experience.

> **Maslow's Hierarchy**
>
> Self-actualization
> Esteem
> Love/belonging
> Safety
> Physiological

We continue to find Maslow's hierarchy (1968) a useful way to think about what happens to people when they are asked to change. Under change-related stress, people may move to a lower level on the hierarchy. With support, they are able to move to higher levels.

First, teachers have survival needs. In that level, teachers are concerned with issues such as: *What is my assignment? Will I have the materials I need to succeed in the classroom?* Once those needs are satisfied, you'll want to turn your attention to security needs. These include: *Will I be successful and appreciated by my principal and colleagues? How will I balance my work and personal life?* Third, teachers have belonging needs. In this stage, they ask questions such as: *Will I enjoy working with my colleagues?* Closely linked to belonging are those related to esteem, such as: *Will parents and/or students think I am a good teacher?*

Once all those needs are satisfied, you can move to working with the need for knowledge. Teachers are interested in topics such as: *What should instruction look like? How to plan a lesson? How to incorporate scaffolding into lessons? Grading and assessment strategies?* Last, after teachers are satisfied with knowledge, they can move to understanding and self-actualization. Note that some authors believe that Maslow's work is best used when you consider it not as a step-by-step approach but as something in which you may need to move back and forth between levels to meet needs, and those needs may change based upon the situation or context.

Need as Identified by Maslow	*Example of Staff Needs*
Aesthetic need (self-actualization)	Attention to the needs of students first.
Need for understanding	Focus on the developmental needs of students.
Need for knowledge	Professional development: Program models Planning skills Curriculum Instructional strategies Diversity issues Assessment strategies
Esteem needs	Will I be successful? Will I be valued?
Belonging needs	Will I fit in? How can I connect with others?
Security needs	Where will I be working? Where will my room or office be located? What will my work look like? Who's making these decisions?
Survival needs	Will I continue to have a job? Will I have the skills for the job? Will I have sufficient and appropriate materials?

Extrinsic and Intrinsic Motivation

There are two main types of motivation: extrinsic and intrinsic. Extrinsic motivation includes all the outside ways we try to influence an adult, such as rewards, bonuses, or extra planning time. Intrinsic motivation comes from within the adult.

With extrinsic rewards, we can get temporary results, but for long-term impact, we need to help adults activate their intrinsic motivation.

It's similar to looking at the ocean. Barbara loves watching the waves but, when doing so, only sees the surface. She can't see the perilous undercurrents. Similarly, extrinsic motivation looks good, but we don't notice the dangers. The true beauty of the ocean is underneath the surface. As we go deeper, there are beautiful marine creatures, fish, and coral. Instead of short-lived waves, she can see long-lasting beauty. And that is intrinsic motivation.

Extrinsic Motivation

Extrinsic motivation is that which comes from outside an adult—anything that is external.

Examples of Extrinsic Rewards

Reward certificates
Positive evaluations
Bonus planning time
Pay increases

Positive Aspects of Extrinsic Motivation

Some authors, such as Alfie Kohn, believe there is never an appropriate use for external motivation, whether for children or adults. Based on our experiences, we believe there are appropriate uses for it. For example, we agree with Daniel Pink (2009), author of *Drive*, who compares extrinsic motivation to caffeine, noting it gets you going (although you are less motivated later).

Larry Ferlazzo, in *Self-Driven Learning* (2013), also points out that everyone needs some baseline rewards, such as a clean classroom, a caring teacher, engaging lessons, and fair grading, in order to be motivated to learn. We can translate that to aspects teachers need, such as a caring and supportive leader, appropriate material and time-based resources, and fair personnel processes. And Daniel Pink also points out that extrinsic rewards do work for a short time for mechanical, rote tasks.

Negative Aspects of Extrinsic Motivation

> **Negative Aspects of Extrinsic Motivation?**
>
> Temporary/constant increase of reward
> Decreases intrinsic motivation?
> Lose internal strengths

There is, however, a downside to extrinsic motivation. The results are most often temporary. To keep adults motivated, while relying on extrinsic motivation, you must continue to increase the reward. That's especially true with things like salary increases. A big increase feels good but is quickly forgotten, and another increase is sought.

A final negative aspect of extrinsic motivation is that people can come to believe that things are out of their control. I'll only get a good evaluation if I always agree with the principal, or I must agree with the department chair if I want a good schedule.

Effective Ways to Use Extrinsic Motivation

"But," you may be thinking, "my adults expect rewards. I can't just not use them!" So how can you effectively use extrinsic rewards? I think it's important to go back to Larry Ferlazzo's comments about baseline rewards and Maslow's hierarchy of needs. For all adults, we need to provide:

- ♦ A clean, safe, caring environment
- ♦ Adequate materials and supplies for everyone

- ♦ Clear and fair evaluations
- ♦ Openness to all ideas and suggestions

In addition, when using extrinsic rewards, we should emphasize the feeling that accompanies the reward, reinforcing that the true reward is how you feel about your success. In other words, move from a reward to celebrating the experience.

There are three other specific tips for using extrinsic motivation. First, when using rewards, do so unannounced. Rather than saying, "If then, then this," simply choose random times to reward adults. By surprising adults, they are encouraged to put forth effort all the time.

Next, reward adults through affirmation of their work. Give them an authentic audience who can appreciate their quality work.

Third, when you are using rewards, make them appropriate and meaningful to the adult. Some adults like certificates; others prefer public recognition. It's also important to be respectful of the individual. Some adults do not like to be singled out in front of their peers. If you know that, find another way to praise them: a note, an individual comment, or even a look.

Reflection Point: How have you used extrinsic motivation effectively with your teachers?

Intrinsic Motivation

Intrinsic motivation is that which comes from within the adult. It is internal as opposed to external. With intrinsic motivation, adults appreciate learning for its own sake. They enjoy learning and the feelings of accomplishment that accompany the activity. There are many benefits to intrinsic motivation. Adults tend to prefer challenging work, are more confident about their abilities, and are confident their ideas and suggestions will be listened to.

The Foundational Elements of Intrinsic Motivation

Intrinsic motivation has two foundational elements: people are more motivated when they value what they are doing and when they believe they have a chance for success. Adults see value in a variety of ways, but the main three are relevance, autonomy, and relationships.

Value

Adults typically see value through the relevance of the tasks they are asked to do, whether that is teaching a lesson, attending a professional development, or completing paperwork. In fact, most adults have a streaming music station playing in their heads, WII-FM—what's in it for me? With the myriad of responsibilities teachers have, they want to pay attention to tasks or content that is relevant to them.

When Barbara does workshops with teachers, she knows they come into her session with one burning question: "How can I use this information immediately?" Adults are juggling so many demands; they prioritize activities and their attention based on how well something meets their immediate needs.

Next, there is value in the autonomy a teacher has. We've talked to teachers who say, "I'm told what to do, how to do it, and when to do it! I'm a teacher, and I know what I am doing. When do I get to decide something?" That is actually a fairly common perception from teachers. As we said earlier, teachers are bound by many mandates, whether related to legalities, curriculum, instruction, or assessment. Although there are some non-negotiables you deal with, if you will find options for teachers to make decisions, you can encourage autonomy and intrinsic motivation.

Ways to Increase Teacher Autonomy

Involve in planning and decision-making.
Provide professional development and support based on their interests and needs.
Balance direction and support.
Provide appropriate recognition.
Communicate to build trust.

Finally, adults find value in their relationships, with you and their peers. Barbara once heard a speaker say that leader and peer relationships are foundational to everything else that happens in the school. That is true. The old adage "They don't care what you know until they know how much you care" is true. Adults need to feel liked, cared for, and respected by their leaders. Many adults also need the same from their peers. If they feel isolated from other teachers, they are disengaged and less likely to see value in what they are doing.

> Reflection Point: How do you already activate the value aspect of intrinsic motivation with your teachers?

Success

Adults are also motivated when they believe they have a chance to be successful. And that belief is built on four building blocks: level of challenge, experiences, encouragement, and views about success.

First, the degree of alignment between the difficulty of an activity and an adult's skill level is a major factor in self-motivation. Imagine that you enjoy playing soccer and you have the chance to compete in a local game. You will be playing against Lionel Messi (Argentina and Barcelona), named World Player of the Year a record six times. How do you feel? In that situation, there's plenty of opportunity for challenge, probably too much challenge! Or perhaps you love reading novels, but the only language you can read is Spanish. How motivated will you be in a literature class? For optimal motivation, the activity should be challenging but in balance with your ability to perform. Part of your job as a leader is to determine if a teacher is struggling and, if so, to provide appropriate support. On the other hand, if one of your teachers is not challenged, look for ways to give them an opportunity to try a new challenge.

> **Opportunities for New Challenges for Teachers**
>
> Identify leadership roles they may assume.
> Ask for assistance with social media strategies.
> Look for district-wide opportunities to share their learning.
> Select them to be a mentor to a new teacher.

Just as we've discussed in many other areas, an adult's experiences are an important factor. A teacher is more likely to believe they can be successful if each of their students graduated at the end of the year. On the other hand, if a teacher found that a large percentage of their students are still reading below grade level, they may feel they failed as a reading teacher.

A third building block to feelings of success is the encouragement an adult receives from others. Encouragement is "the process of facilitating the development of the person's inner resources and courage towards positive movement" (Dinkmeyer & Losoncy, 1980, p. 16).

When you encourage, you accept teachers as they are, so they will accept themselves. You value and reinforce attempts and efforts and help them realize that mistakes are learning tools. Encouragement says, "Try, and try again. You can do it. Go in your own direction, at your own pace. I believe in you." Encouragement can be in the form of words, but you can also provide encouragement through a consistent, positive presence in your teachers' lives.

It's also important for adults to read and learn about people who failed before they succeeded, because the final building block is an adult's views about success and failure. Many adults see failure as the end rather than as an opportunity to learn before trying again. But there are countless examples, from Abraham Lincoln to Steve Jobs, of people who have experienced

Reflection Point: How do you already activate the success aspect of intrinsic motivation with your teachers?

failure in their lives, only to become successful. How you define success and failure drives many of your beliefs about your own ability to succeed.

Final Thoughts

Everyone is motivated, just not motivated in the same way, or by the same things. This chapter examined both kinds of motivation, extrinsic and intrinsic, and provided strategies and suggestions for how school leaders recognize the motivation of their teachers. The remaining chapters will look at specific motivational strategies leaders can employ to improve both motivation and morale in their school.

2

Growth Mindset and Resilience

> Motivation Connection: Growth mindset and resilience are both reflections of intrinsic motivation. Feelings related to value (relevance, autonomy, and relationships) and success are woven throughout the two.

Healthy schools, schools with high morale and highly motivated teachers, are places where there is a growth mindset and where the staff are resilient. But that focus, and that resilience, doesn't come naturally. It emerges when the school leader understands the importance of both and how they can positively impact student learning. It emerges when leaders possess a growth mindset for their teachers, and other employees, and when leaders themselves do the things that cultivate resilience.

This chapter will examine the concept of growth mindset and resilience and provide explicit steps and strategies that leaders can use to assure their school is a place where teachers want to work and families want to send their children to learn.

Fixed Mindset vs. Growth Mindset

There is a difference between a fixed mindset and a growth mindset. As Carol Dweck explains, a fixed mindset assumes that our character, intelligence, and creative ability are static and cannot be changed. A growth mindset, on the other hand, adopts the perspective that our intelligence, creativity, and character can change and grow over time.

These two views have a tremendous impact on teaching and learning. If a teacher believes in a fixed mindset, then he or she is saying there is no potential for growth. If a child is intelligent, they will continue to be so. If a child is struggling, it's because he or she just isn't "smart enough." On the other hand, if you believe in a growth mindset, you believe that students may start with a certain amount of ability but that can change over time with effort and persistence.

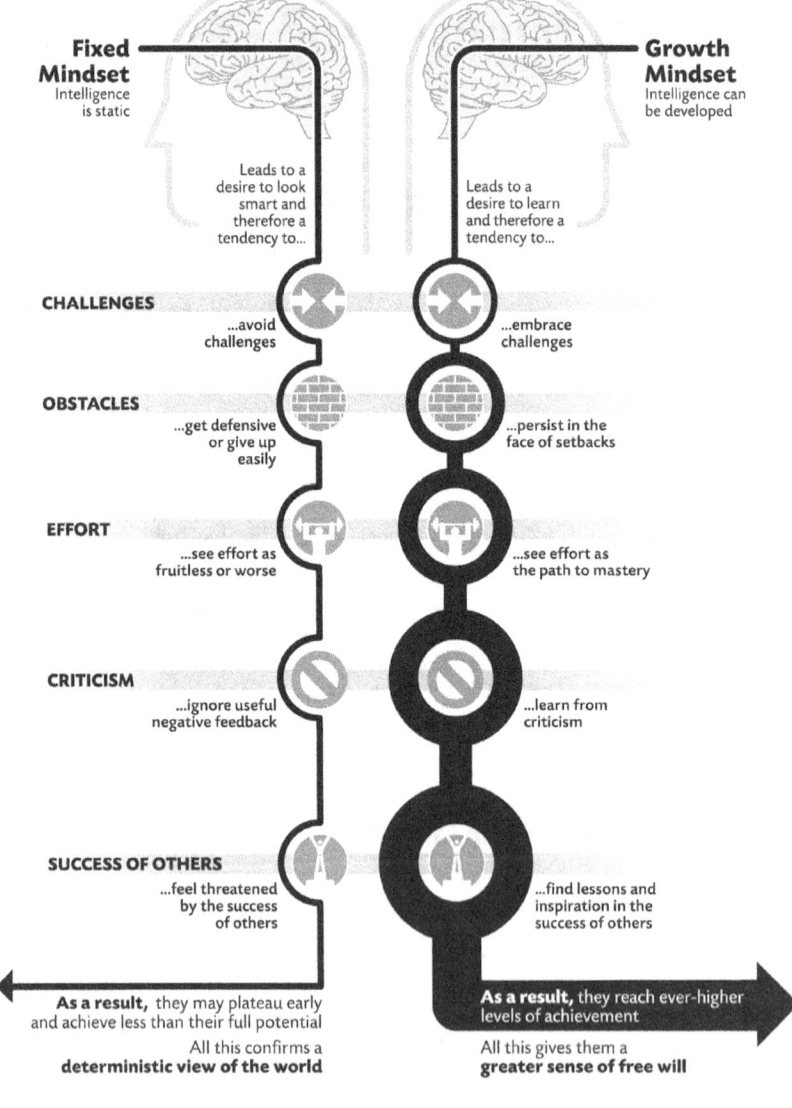

For students, which of these they believe also matters. Students with a fixed mindset typically avoid challenges, feel threatened by others' successes, and give up easily. They want to look smart, and believe that working hard at a task means they are not smart.

Students with a growth mindset believe they can learn and become better. They embrace challenge, view effort as a positive part of learning, and persist through difficulties. Nigel Holmes provides a clear breakdown of the two mindsets discovered by Dr. Dweck. As you read the table, see if you can identify these traits in your struggling learners.

Strategies to Develop a Growth Mindset in Your School

A growth mindset is critical to a learning-focused school. After all, if you don't believe a student can learn and grow, what difference can you make? During the remainder of this section, we'll look at six strategies to develop a growth mindset in your school.

Strategies to Develop a Growth Mindset in Your School

- Build a learning-oriented mindset.
- Try new things.
- Collaborate.
- Emphasize mastery and learning.
- Focus on feedback and reflection.
- Own mistakes and talk about them.

Build a Learning-Oriented Mindset

The very heart of a growth mindset is an orientation toward learning. Growth requires learning. There are several ways to build a learning mindset in your school. First, make your focus clear, through your words and actions. Explain a learning-oriented mindset and reinforce it in newsletters, emails, and meetings. One principal we worked with created a new tagline for his school: *Ledbetter School Is All About Learning*.

It's also important to hold teachers accountable for improvement. Talk with them about what they've recently learned. Ask them to share with you, and with others. Reinforce improvement continually. Finally, Barbara worked with one principal who wanted his teachers to focus on learning during decision-making. They created a poster for his door.

> How does _____
> positively impact student learning?

Anytime a teacher asked him for something, whether it was funding for a new resource, time for professional development, or a student activity, they were asked to justify their request based on learning. The principal later shared with Barbara that, over time, this made a difference in how they approached decision-making.

Try New Things

Too often, without meaning to, we discourage teachers from trying new things. Consider a faculty meeting where these comments were overheard.

> That's a good idea. We should try it later.
> We've never done it that way.
> I don't think our budget will allow that.
> I tried that before, and it didn't work.

Does that sound familiar? If we want teachers to innovate, we need to provide a culture that supports innovation. Leaders need to model openness to new ideas. This includes being open and available to your teachers, listening (see chapter 4) without immediately rendering judgment, and asking questions to help them clarify their ideas.

Leaders who are open to new ideas provide support in trying new things. This may include financial, physical, or human resources. Barbara worked with a middle school where a new teacher wanted to implement cooperative learning for his students. However, he was worried he would be reprimanded for issues with classroom management. The principal worked with the curriculum facilitator, the assistant principal, and the teacher of special-needs students to provide assistance with the management of groups. As the day progressed, the teacher thanked the others for their help and, one at a time, asked them to leave. He gradually increased his own leadership and management and, by the end of the day, was solely responsible for the lesson. As he told the principal, "I wouldn't have been able to do it had you not provided help. I was able to wade into the new type of lesson rather than jumping in the deep end."

Collaborate

The opportunity to collaborate is important when supporting a growth mindset. Groups, when structured appropriately and when following collaborative norms, are more likely to focus on growth and positive movement. Let's think about it this way: In groups that are focused on a fixed mindset, they focus on the past, use checklists for tasks, and celebrate individual accomplishments. With a growth mindset, different perspectives are celebrated, there is a culture of trust that everyone is contributing to the group goal, and the overall focus is on impacting others. As you think about this comparison and compare it to aspects of your culture, you'll see that growth mindset–oriented collaboration benefits your faculty and staff and students.

Carol Dweck points out, "When entire companies embrace a growth mindset, their employees report feeling more empowered and committed; they also receive far greater organizational support for collaboration and innovation" (https://hbr.org/2016/01/what-having-a-growth-mindset-actually-means).

Emphasize Mastery and Learning

Across the nation, many schools have a focus on achievement rather than growth. If you work in a state that mandates that type of focus, it's difficult to adjust the focus. However, it's critical to provide options for teachers to emphasize mastery and learning rather than focusing on test scores or completing a task. We recommend the use of *lesson studies*, which provide an opportunity for collaboration and reflection. Originally used by Japanese teachers, lesson studies emphasize working in small groups to plan, teach, observe, and critique a lesson. A lesson study involves groups of teachers in a collaborative process designed to systematically examine their practice, with the goal of becoming more effective, which inherently focuses on growth mindset. The lesson study protocol describes the process itself; the lesson study observation is a blank observational form you may want to use or adapt.

Lesson Study Protocol

- Participants should be volunteers, but the invitation to participate should be inclusive.
- While working on a study lesson, teachers work together to develop a detailed plan for the lesson.
- One member of the group teaches the lesson in a real classroom while other members of the group observe the lesson.
- The group comes together to discuss their observations about the lesson and student learning.
- The group works together to revise the lesson.
- Another teacher teaches the revised lesson while group members observe.
- The group reconvenes to discuss the observed lesson.
- The revision process may continue as long as the group believes it is necessary.
- Teachers talk about what the study lesson taught them and how they can apply the learning to their own classroom. They may prepare a report to be shared with others.

Lesson Study Observation

Participant observer:	Date:
Grade/level:	Subject:
Objective:	
Observations/notes about content of lesson:	
Observations/notes about pacing of lesson:	
Observations/notes about student engagement:	
Other observations/notes/questions:	

Additional information about conducting a lesson study is available from Education Northwest at https://educationnorthwest.org/sites/default/files/lesson-study-participant-guide.pdf.

Focus on Feedback and Reflection

As you consider the aspects of growth mindset we've discussed so far, you'll notice that reflection and feedback are a part of each. Both components are foundational to growth mindset, and you'll want to make sure they are not only integral to your efforts but that you also positively reinforce teachers' incorporation of each. In addition to their use during observations and during post-observation conferences, always encourage teachers to reflect on their work. The ability to self-diagnose their work, to reinforce what worked, and to adjust what didn't is an important part of reflection.

> **Sample Reflective Questions**
>
> An effective part of the lesson was . . .
> Students responded well to . . .
> Students struggled with . . .
> I was surprised by . . .
> I would adapt . . .
> I would keep . . .
> I've learned xxx about your son/daughter . . .

You might think about asking teachers to send you a short weekly email using the following prompts.

> This week . . .
> I learned . . .
> I was encouraged by . . .

Own Mistakes and Talk about Them

Finally, it's important for your teachers to talk about things that didn't go well and own their part of them. One school we worked with had a section of their electronic management resource called "Educational Encounters." Teachers posted new ideas they learned and implemented, as well as what happened. You might imagine that the successes generated the most discussion, but the opposite occurred. Once teachers began to share about their failures, other teachers were encouraging and enthusiastic about how everyone could learn from the mistakes. Another school used a similar method in the faculty workroom, calling it "Marvelous Mistakes." The focus was on how to learn from the experience, not the fact that something didn't work.

Assess Yourself

Element	I'm Okay But Need to Work on This Area	I Think I Do a Satisfactory Job	I Go Over and Above in This Area	Evidence for Your Assessment
Build a learning-oriented mindset.				
Try new things.				
Collaborate.				
Emphasize mastery and learning.				
Focus on feedback and reflection.				
Own mistakes and talk about them.				

Resilience

Winston Churchill once said, "Success is not final, failure is not fatal: it is the courage to continue that counts." That's what resilience is about. Resilience is that "something" that helps us deal effectively with pressure, to bounce back from failure and address and positively overcome everyday challenges. It is a critical part of growth mindset and is essential to teachers' successes, especially in a challenging environment.

Strategies for Building Resilience

Be empathetic with yourself.
Change negative scripts.
Set realistic expectations and goals.
Recognize that mistakes are something to learn from.
Reinforce our "islands of competence."
Practice effective problem-solving.

Be Empathetic with Yourself

Adults who are resilient are empathetic toward themselves. They treat themselves with the same grace and encouragement they would use with their best friends. In other words, if they make a mistake or fail, they "cut themselves a break." For a teacher, this might mean accepting that when a lesson doesn't work, that is normal, and one should learn from it and move on. However, many teachers blame themselves anytime they are not perfect, and they obsess over mistakes. When this happens, it can be difficult for teachers to readjust and focus on progress. When encouraging resilience with your teachers, model self-empathy, be empathetic, and share empathy strategies with your teachers.

> Practice kindness toward yourself.
> Practice mindfulness.
> Don't compare yourself to others.
> Focus on the positive.

Changing "Negative Scripts"

Teachers who are not resilient typically have a negative script running in their heads at all times. In their minds, they hear comments like, "You're not good enough," or "You shouldn't have tried." It's important for us, as leaders, to address this with our struggling teachers and help them reframe the negatives as positives. As with empathy, positive scripts help teachers focus on progress, which, in turn, leads to increased student achievement. One specific strategy is that, during post-observation conferences, help teachers turn any negative scripts and comments into positive ones.

Negative	*Positive*
This was the worst lesson I've taught.	This lesson wasn't ideal. I've learned . . . .
I'm never going to succeed.	I can tell I'm making progress.
The lesson just didn't work.	This lesson didn't work the way I wanted, but I did learn . . .
I just want to be perfect.	If I never fail, I'll never learn.

Set Realistic Expectations and Goals

Although people who are resilient have high expectations for themselves, they are also realistic. For example, Jenny, a teacher who has high yet realistic goals, might desire to be an excellent teacher who is recognized for her work. In this case, her expectations are based on her desire to make a difference, but also on her knowledge of her strengths as a teacher. What she didn't do is set herself up for failure, setting a goal of being awarded the National Teacher of the Year, something over which she has no control.

As a leader, it's important to help your teachers set realistic goals. You probably already have a structure for goal-setting; simply ensure expectations that are practical. Encourage your teachers by setting and sharing your own realistic goals, providing guidelines and samples if needed, and giving positive feedback and support.

Sample Goals

Improve pacing of lessons.
Incorporate differentiation in lessons.
Develop and implement a PD plan for teaching students with special needs.
Expand the role of parents in classroom.
Earn national board certification.
Enroll and attend a graduate class on instructional methods in science.

Recognizing That You Can Learn from Mistakes

Earlier, we mentioned that one way to help students build resilience is to help them recognize that mistakes help you learn. How students view mistakes reflects how they feel about failure. For example, we all know people who have made a mistake or failed in some way, learned a lesson, and later became successful.

It's important for us to deal with failure in a positive manner. There are four steps you can take to do so.

1. Remind yourself, and teachers, of others (famous people, people from literature, local role models) who have failed but later succeeded.
2. Share your own stories of what you have learned from mistakes, as well as telling stories (anonymously) of other teachers who have been successful. Encourage them to share their own stories.
3. Treat each mistake as a learning opportunity. Focus on the positive and how we can grow in the future.
4. Constantly and consistently reinforce that mistakes and failures are a natural part of learning.

Reinforce Islands of Competence

In order to build resilience, you also need to reinforce islands of competence, or those areas in which you and your teachers are skilled. In any job, there are a variety of roles, but those who are resilient find ways to maximize their skilled areas. For example, on a team of teachers, you may have one that is particularly effective with parents, another who likes to organize, and a third who enjoys researching new ideas. To build on their islands of competence, have them collaborate on tasks for the entire team, with one coordinating parent communication, another handling paperwork, and the third researching new instructional ideas. What this particular principal found was that, by focusing on areas of strength (and interest), the three teachers maximized their effectiveness as a team.

You may not be aware of the islands of competence of all your teachers. Or you may have teachers who say, "I'm good at everything." However, if your teachers are aware of their strengths and build on them, they are more likely to be resilient during challenges.

Quick Questions

What is your favorite part of teaching? Why? What is an example of that?

What is your least favorite part of your job? Why? What is an example of that?

Practice Effective Problem-Solving

Finally, to build resilience, you need to use effective problem-solving strategies. That may sound like common sense, but during a challenging time, we may try to simply guess the best option or make an emotional decision. If your teachers are facing a challenge, it's even more important to use problem-solving strategies. It's more effective to focus on possible solutions, the possible advantages and disadvantages, and the best option for progress.

Problem	
Possible Solution 1	
Advantages	Disadvantages
Possible Solution 2	
Advantages	Disadvantages
Possible Solution 3	
Advantages	Disadvantages

As a leader, model using effective problem-solving and encourage your teachers to use the same strategies. Additionally, when teachers are struggling, gently remind them to focus on the problem and research-based strategies rather than doing what is simplest or quickest.

Assess Yourself

Element	I'm Okay but Need to Work on This Area	I Think I Do a Satisfactory Job	I Go Over and Above in This Area	Evidence for Your Assessment
Be empathetic with yourself.				
Be empathetic with yourself.				
Collaborate.				
Set realistic expectations and goals.				
Recognize that mistakes are something to learn from.				
Reinforce "islands of competence."				
Practice effective problem-solving.				

Final Thoughts

To improve morale and motivation, it's critical that the leader possess a growth mindset for both teachers and students. When they do so, they model behaviors that reinforce the positive traits associated with growth, and they will learn that their behavior can cultivate resilience among their staff.

3

A School's Reputation

The Intersection Between Climate and Culture

Motivation Connection: Teachers feel more valued and successful working in a school that has an authentic, positive reputation, which reflects the school's culture.

Does a school have a reputation? How about a principal? A teacher? A school district? Of course they do. Despite common rhetoric which often claims schools are similar, or all teachers are equally good, there is a difference among schools, principals, and teachers.

That's not a bad thing. In fact, we suggest that schools, and teachers and principals, are most effective when they reflect the unique needs of their students and their community.

But reputations can be both helpful and detrimental to the success of a school. Reputations can also positively or negatively impact the motivations of your teachers. This chapter will explore the most essential things that contribute to a school's reputation and will provide suggestions for how a principal,

Reflection Point: What is the reputation of your school?

and their staff, can assure that their school has a positive image in educational community and their community at large.

Climate and Culture

The terms "school climate" and "school culture" are often used interchangeably to describe how people view a school, its programs, and its personnel. We'll provide a brief overview of the two concepts and then discuss how they intersect to shape a school's reputation.

School Climate

School climate and culture are distinct. The climate of a school most often is a description of the "feel" or "tone" of the school, the relationships among teachers and other staff, between school personnel and parents and the community, and the overall motivation and morale of the setting.

As such, *climate* is often a description of the current tenor of the school and can reflect underlying tensions and concerns about student learning, curricular changes, or student safety. Because climate is rather amorphous, it often changes based on local events, but it can be shaped by larger community or societal trends.

A recent example of how climate shifts occurred as schools grappled with COVID and its impact on their program. Schools that were known for their stellar communication with parents and their open, engaging campus were suddenly seen differently as schools shifted to remote learning and campuses became more closed. Often, the communication strategies that were previously successful were now seen as outdated and ineffective. In many cases, schools were seen as less effective and less responsive.

Reflection Point: How would you describe the climate of your school?

School Culture

School culture is different in that it reflects deeply held sets of values, traditions, and patterns of behavior that are present. Those values and beliefs are so embedded in the day-to-day activity of school personnel and the community that they are simply accepted as the normal "way we do things" in our school.

Culture reflects the often-unspoken and unwritten norms about a school and can heavily influence motivation. Influential staff members, teachers, or administrators, and whom others recognize as leaders and opinion makers, often transmit the culture from generation to generation. As the staff changes, the cultural norms get passed along, and the culture often stays the same.

School culture can manifest itself in the day-to-day routines and activities in a school. That can include routine activities, like the way students are welcomed, or how lunch is organized. It's reflected in decisions about budget priorities, which teachers or students are recognized, openness to creativity or reliance on compliance, and even the provision of professional development.

Culture is also amorphous and rather intangible. But it can be seen in things like rituals and ceremonies, the stories that are shared about a school, or who gets recognized and rewarded.

Indicators of School Culture

- Stories and tales are recollections of events that are told and retold. They are a powerful way to share examples of values and beliefs. Most stories contain a moral lesson and are inevitably engaging.
- Rituals, routines, and ceremonies provide structure to daily activity in a school. Rituals occur regularly, while ceremonies are often grander and less frequent. Routines, like how students are welcomed into a building or organized for dismissal, reflect underlying values. Ceremonies, like graduation, carry meaning and reflect values and norms about what is important.
- Heroes and heroines are present in every school. They are the people who are most admired and looked up to by others. The examples can be both positive and negative. Regardless, they reflect beliefs about what is valued.
- Rewards and reinforcements also reflect what is valued and, therefore, rewarded. What values do students and teachers that are recognized represent? Does policy value compliance or creativity?

Source: Adapted from Bolman and Deal (2021) and Peterson and Deal (2009).

Assess Yourself

	Guiding Questions	Examples from Your School
Rituals and ceremonies	♦ What are the routines and rituals in your school? What values do they represent? ♦ Are there special ceremonies or events at your school? What do they celebrate? ♦ What messages do you communicate in your daily actions, classroom visits, and other interactions with members of your school community?	
Heroes and heroines	♦ Who are the heroes or heroines on your staff? Why are they recognized? ♦ What ways do you identify and celebrate people who contribute to the success of every student? Who have high expectations for student success?	
Stories and tales	♦ How do you communicate verbally and through your actions with your faculty and staff? What underlying messages are represented? ♦ What are the stories you tell about your school, its students, and its staff? What stories do you encourage others to tell?	
Rewards and reinforcements	♦ How do you recognize and reward teachers? What values are recognized and rewarded? Are these strategies successful? ♦ Do you routinely reward teachers, staff, and students who make exceptional efforts to improve student learning?	

Because culture reflects deeply held beliefs and values, often those shared with the community, it's often more complex to modify. But there are things that leaders can do to shape the culture of their school or district.

Ways to Shape Culture

- Develop a set of stories about student, and teacher, success. Use every opportunity to share those stories with teachers, families, and community. Add to your collection regularly.
- Consider how you spend time every day. Maximize the time you spend in classrooms. Find time to talk with teachers about their instruction and how you can be supportive. What you pay attention to becomes important in your school.
- Think about how you respond to critical incidents and events. Your behavior will model how teachers and other staff respond.
- Think about how students and teachers are recognized. Make sure every recognition is authentic, is individualized, and supports your school's mission and vision.
- Value professional learning. Attend along with your teachers. Join book study groups, team meetings. Talk about what you've learned or recently read. Encourage others to share their learning.
- Recognize your influence as a role model. Your presence, or absence, in the school signals your priorities. The way you talk with teachers about their work lets them know what is valued.
- Think about your school's budget. How are funds allocated for materials, professional learning, and other items? Assure the budget supports your school's vision and mission.
- Identify ways to expand your presence in your school community. What groups might you meet with or speak to about your school? How can you spread the good news about your students and teachers?

What Does This Have to Do with Our Reputation?

Both a school's culture, it's long-standing beliefs and actions, as well as a school's climate, current perceptions about effectiveness and relationships, contribute to a school's reputation. Among parents, community, or even among teachers, there is little distinction. The two work together to shape opinion about your school, and people will act based upon those beliefs.

Successful principals recognize the power of both climate and culture to shape their school. They are skilled at linking everyday practices in ways that reinforce the school's values and mission.

So what does a leader do? How do you make sure your school is a place where parents are comfortable enrolling their children, and a place where teachers, and other employees, are motivated to work?

It Starts with Vision

The most effective leaders have a clear vision for their school. Being clear about your personal vision is one of the most important things you can do (Fullan, 2015).

While personal vision is essential, a shared vision, one developed collaboratively with teachers, other staff, and community, is even more important. That shared vision should guide everything that occurs in the school, from curricular decisions to budgetary priorities, organizational arrangements, and personnel decisions.

Both one's personal vision and the school's shared vision must be more than just words on paper, or a website. It must be a living, breathing document, with broad ownership, and reflects the deepest and most valued beliefs and motivations of your school community.

We don't suggest you, or your school community, develop a vision statement every year, but if you don't have one, or haven't worked on one in a long time, it may be time to revisit your personal and collective, shared vision.

> Reflection Point: What is your personal vision?
> What is the shared vision in your school?

Even in schools with a clear vision statement, it is important to revisit and recommit to that vision. Like most things in our lives, our work setting changes. Schools change all the time. Staff retire, and replacements are hired. Families move, and new ones enroll. Our school communities change a little each and every year. It's often critical to revisit the vision and assure it aligns with the current reality.

Personal Vision

Describing one's personal vision is not easy. Because it reflects our most intimate beliefs about life and about our work, preparing a statement of personal vision can be incredibly difficult. In their book on ethical leadership and decision-making, Joan Shapiro and Jacqueline Stefkovich (2021) describe work on a personal vision, or ethic, as one of the most important things a leader can do to be clear about what they value and about what is important in their school.

A Personal Vision

Your personal vision consists of the most fundamental beliefs you hold about life, about your work, and about relationships with people. A four-step process can be used to think about your own personal vision for your school.

Developing a Personal Vision

Step 1 Think about your school. Make a list of what you would like to achieve as you work on improvement. Describe what it looks like and feels like.

Step 2 Consider the following things about what you have written: relationships, personal interests, and community. Examine each item in your list to ensure that it still fits.

Step 3 Develop a list of priorities. Identify the most important. Once this is done, review the list and rank them from most to least important. Remove the least important. Re-rank if appropriate. Check for relevance with your earlier list. Eliminate any item that is not relevant.

Step 4 Use the items from the first three steps to develop a personal vision statement. Review and edit the statement as often as needed until you believe it accurately reflects your commitment to your improvement plan.

Source: Adapted from Williamson and Blackburn (2020).

Develop Your Own

What We Would Like to Achieve	Reflect and Revise on Your List
List Your Priorities	Rank Your Priorities
Personal Vision Statement	

Vision Letters

A personal vision is also important for teachers and others who work in your school. While the beginning of the school year is a good time to invite teachers to consider their own personal vision, it can occur at any time.

In her book on classroom motivation, Barbara (2005) recommends having teachers write vision letters. The letters provide teachers with an opportunity to consider the sort of classroom they want to create.

For example, ask teachers to imagine that it is the last day of school and to write a letter or email to another teacher describing the past year—all that students accomplished, the work in their classroom, ways they supported student learning. Then ask teachers to describe how they plan to achieve their vision.

One principal we worked with asks teachers to write a vision letter at the start of every school year. Several times during the year, they are asked to look at the letter and think about their progress toward making the vision a reality. This principal says that it is a "really helpful motivational tool."

Another way to use the vision letter is to have teachers write the letter to you as principal. You can then use the letter as a part of a conversation with each teacher about his or her vision of a more effective classroom and how it relates to your vision of a more effective school.

> **A Vision Letter to the Principal**
>
> Ask teachers to imagine that it is the last day of school and the past year was the most successful year of their career. What happened in their classrooms? What happened in the school? How did they grow personally and professionally?

Shared Vision

Possessing a clear and compelling personal vision is important, but not sufficient. Effective principals recognize the importance of working with staff and community to develop, nurture, and sustain a strong, collectively held vision for their school.

When asking people to think about their shared vision, it can be helpful to involve participants in a thoughtful yet engaging activity. One approach is to build on the vision letter activity.

After teachers write their individual visions, have them meet in small groups, such as by grade level, in teams, or in subject area departments. Ask each group to discuss their letters and create a common vision for the small group. Finally, ask small groups to work together as a school faculty to write a shared vision for the school.

Another idea is the "View from a Hot-Air Balloon." The principals we've worked with find this activity a fun way to launch the conversation about vision.

> Imagine you're hovering in a hot-air balloon over your school, and imagine it as good as it might be—what would you see, what would you feel, what would you hear?

At one school, the principal used a two-step process. First, she asked teachers to describe what they would currently see and hear in their school. Then they were asked to imagine it was five years in the future and to describe what they would see and hear from their hot-air balloon in their school as a result of their improvement plan.

Today	Five Years from Today

Creating or Recommitting to a School-Wide Vision

Skillful principals recognize the importance of working with their school community to develop, nurture, and sustain a collectively held vision for their school.

Every school we've visited has a mission or vision statement. Many, however, are out-of-date and rarely used to set goals and priorities, allocate resources, or make decisions about school programs. Even the clearest statements need periodic review. A review allows you to adjust the mission and vision based on up-to-date information about students and their needs. A review also allows the staff "to recommit to the school's core values and beliefs" (Williamson & Blackburn, 2020).

Process for Developing a School Vision Statement

Activity 1   What are the things people are pleased with and frustrated about at this school? (Designed to get the issues on the table.)

Activity 2   Invite the group to consider the values that should guide the school. You might ask, "As we begin planning for our future, what values are most important to you as we create our vision statement?" (Use of "I believe" statements focus on the important things.)
Note: A helpful approach is to have the group read some common things. For example, information about developmental needs of students, future trends, information about recommendations for schools at that level. Often, professional associations (NASSP, ASCD) have useful resources. Shared readings create a common base of information and are particularly useful to minimize the barriers between teachers and parents where parents often defer to teachers as the "experts."

Activity 3   Ask the group to respond to the following: "Imagine it is the year 20XX. We have been able to operationalize our beliefs. What does our school look, sound, and feel like? Describe the vision." (Helps to identify the target the school will work toward.)

Activity 4   In work, groups develop a draft mission statement to be shared with the larger group. (Development of multiple models promotes discussion, clarification, and consensus building.)

Activity 5   Share the drafts, ask questions and seek clarification, and seek consensus on a statement. Plan to share it with the larger school community for feedback and comment.

Source: Williamson and Blackburn (2020).

Vision is one of the most important components of an effective school. Being clear about your personal vision and working with others to be clear about the vision for your school help you and your faculty balance competing demands and make decisions based on your collective vision for your school.

Final Thoughts

The most successful leaders recognize the importance of developing and nurturing a shared vision for their school, one that reflects the values and motivations of teachers. They also know that the vision must guide every decision and every action that they take. When vision aligns with action, it transforms a school. That transformation is what impacts your school's reputation.

Aligning vision with action means that cultural norms may change, and that change will resonate throughout the school community. Over time, it will change the way teachers, families, and community think about your school. But it will do more than change the culture; the evidence is that a school with a clear vision, and actions aligned with that vision, is a place where school climate is improved. Teachers and administrators are more collaborative. There is a commitment to professional learning, and there is a willingness to take risks on behalf of improving the educational experience of students. And it transforms into a place where families want to send their children and teachers and other employees want to work.

4

SCT Effective Support

Listen, Then Build a System

Motivation Connection: To address teachers' values and help them be successful, you need to listen effectively, then build structures that help them.

As mentioned earlier, almost every aspect of our society has become politicized, and that includes schools. Principals are regularly confronted by passionate parents who object to a change in policy, curricular modifications, or even routine school operations. It might be a single highly vocal parent, a subtle chatter on social media, or an organized group advocating for change.

The dilemma for principals is that there often are conflicting demands from different groups of parents, school employees, and community members. Principals are often caught in the middle, and it seems as though no decision can possibly satisfy the conflicting demands.

Reflection Point: Describe a time when there was so much talking it was almost impossible to listen to any one perspective.

It Starts with Listening

Listening is a key skill for every school leader, especially when faced by the need to mediate complex and often-volatile issues. School leaders must often navigate these challenges, and the ability to communicate effectively is essential. Perhaps the most critical communication skill is listening, the ability to authentically hear what is said, keep an open mind, and despite differences, work together on behalf of students.

We've found three principles characterize an effective communicator. With those concepts as a foundation, we've identified five barriers to effective listening and ten tips to help every leader become an effective listener.

> Keep the focus on the speaker, not you.
> Be open to what they say.
> Be willing to change or take action if appropriate.

Assess Yourself

Element	I'm Okay but Need to Work on This Area	I Think I Do a Satisfactory Job	I Go Over and Above in This Area	Evidence for Your Assessment
Focus on Speaker.				
Be open to the speaker's point of view.				
Be willing to change or take action.				

Barriers to Effective Listening

There are five barriers to listening. They're always present but are exacerbated when trying to communicate with people who are aggressive or combative or when faced by a volatile situation.

Indifference

The first barrier is when we are indifferent to the other person, their issues, or their perspective. Repeatedly hearing the same comments, or listening to abusive or volatile language, often leads listeners to indifference. Parents, and teachers, will pick up on that behavior and assume you are dismissive of their concern or not taking their concern seriously. Avoid being indifferent by being attentive, not arguing with the person, and making direct eye contact.

Assumptions

Making assumptions also undermines the ability to clearly communicate. You might assume you already know what a person thinks or how they feel, assuming they have the same background knowledge that you do, or believing they should interpret that knowledge the same way you do. Avoid making assumptions about others. Instead, listen for verbal clues or non-verbal action that offers insights into their thinking.

Distractions

A third obstacle to effective listening are distractions. Distractions include interruptions, multitasking, or anticipating your next comments rather than paying attention to what the speaker is saying. Active listeners focus on the speaker, avoid distractions like calls, emails, or tests, and assure their attention is on the conversation. The solution is actually simple: Stop doing anything else, and patiently listen to the other person. Focus on the speaker, not your own needs.

Hurrying

This actually leads to the fourth obstacle, hurrying the process. This is particularly true if we aren't interested in the other person or his or her concerns. Oftentimes, we want to hurry the process because we've already made up our minds about the urgency of the issue or the resolution. Allow ample time to listen to the speaker. Ask clarifying questions to make sure you have adequate information. As mentioned earlier, avoid distractions and interruptions that convey to the speaker that you are not interested in what they are saying.

Information Overload

The final barrier to effective listening is information overload. Sometimes, we simply want to get our point across, and we overload the other person with too much, or extraneous, information. Don't try to justify a decision by dominating the discussion with long answers or extended rationale. Focus on listening, gathering information, and assuring that the speaker feels validated rather than marginalized.

Assess Yourself

Element	I'm Okay but Need to Work on This Area	I Think I Do a Satisfactory Job	I Go Over and Above in This Area	What I can do to improve
Indifference				
Assumptions				
Distractions				
Hurrying				
Information overload				

Begin with a Mental Adjustment

Access to school leaders is easy. Parents and others know how to get attention. Use social media. Send emails or texts. Post on a local news site like NextDoor. How do you respond?

It's often helpful to start with our own thoughts. They drive our feelings and actions. Therefore, adjust your mental process and how you think about those who complain or raise issues about your school.

Negative Thoughts	*Positive Thoughts*
It's impossible to keep everyone happy.	Every interaction I have with people will be sincere, regardless of their behavior.
I'm tired of hearing the same issues.	I will actively listen to every person who wishes to speak with me.
I'll never be able to respond to all these texts or emails.	Every day I will strive to respond to every message I receive.
I'm tired of people making assumptions about our teachers and our school.	I will only use data to discuss issues about my school.

Copyright material from Ronald Williamson and Barbara R. Blackburn (2024), *Improving Teacher Morale and Motivation: Leadership Strategies that Build Student Success,* Routledge

After Listening, Act

Listening is important, but then it's important to take further actions. Let's look at two areas.

> Actions that improve communication
> What a leader can do

Actions that Improve Communication

Most of us have experienced times when we felt we were not listened to, which heavily impacts motivation. While you can't manage the behaviors of others, there are specific steps you can take to improve your listening skills and contribute to more effective communication. Over the past 30 years, we've talked to thousands of school leaders and identified ten specific skills that will improve your listening. Many of us already use some of or all these skills. What is critical is to make them a routine part of our leadership repertoire so that we assure their use, particularly when dealing with a challenging or volatile situation.

- Make eye contact.
- Use positive body language.
- Restate or affirm what the other person is saying.
- Ask clarifying questions to help you understand the information.
- Wait to share your comment until the other person is finished.
- Pause and allow silence if appropriate.
- Be fully present and avoid distractions.
- Keep an open mind.
- React to the content, not the person. Never personalize the issue.
- If you choose to take notes, inform the other person and explain why. That way, they don't think you are ignoring them.

What a Leader Can Do

When faced with conflicting parental, or community, demands, what does a leader do? How might you respond? What longer-term strategies might you adopt? Here are proven strategies that will help you lessen the impact of conflict with parent and community groups.

> *Recognize the Value of Critics.* No one enjoys being criticized or having their school, or their policies, attacked. Ron worked for a superintendent who often talked about critics as friends—friends, because they often pointed out gaps in our thinking or provided alternatives to be considered. Understand that the presence of critics doesn't negate what you've done. But listening to the issues may offer strategies for strengthening and enhancing policy and practice. Listening is often the most important response, especially if you are respectful and empathetic.
>
> *Remain Calm.* Always show that you take criticism well. Don't get emotional or angry. When a leader loses their "cool," they lose control of the discussion and demonstrate lack of interest in others' points of view.
>
> *Be Respectful and Courteous.* It's so very important for a leader to be respectful of all members of their school community. Even when you disagree, it's important to carefully choose the words that frame your response, to use terms that calm rather than inflame, and to be attentive to the tone of your response. That can be difficult when the other party doesn't adhere to those guidelines, but it is critical for the leader to model behavior and language that moderate the discussion.
>
> *Engage in Skillful Listening.* As we discussed earlier, listening is often the most critical skill of a leader. When conflict is present, listening can demonstrate that you take the issue seriously, that you respect the person or group you're dealing with, and that you want to learn more about their concern and suggestions. A challenge is that skillful listening can be misinterpreted by your critics and they may believe that you agree with their position. That's why it's important to also be inquisitive and

ask questions that demonstrate interest in learning more, but not necessarily agreeing with their position.

Be Inquisitive and Curious. Things almost always go better when a leader is recognized for their skill at open communication. Skillful listeners demonstrate a genuine interest in what the other person has to say, even your fiercest critics. At the same time, be inquisitive. Ask clarifying questions. Don't be accusatory. When you remain open, you keep learning. Use paraphrasing to show that you are listening and understand what was said.

Speak Like a Real Person. A critical part of inquisitiveness and promoting further discussion is to avoid educational jargon. People don't like those who think they know more or are smarter than they are. Talk like a real person and use everyday words.

Dig Deeper. We'll discuss this again, but always take a close look at what may be contributing to the behavior or concern. Often, it's not the issue that appears to be on the surface. We're not suggesting deep analysis of the issues but to listen for clues about things that may contribute to the conflict. Critics often feel that they are not listened to and that they, or their children, are not served well. Listen for clues about people or events that may have triggered the response. Avoid emotional reactions to their responses.

Part of digging deeper is asking open-ended questions that promote discussion. Solutions emerge not from emotional responses but from information and data. One way to gather that data is to ask clarifying questions. Never make accusations or limit conversation. Effective leaders don't judge a person's motives by criticizing or labeling; instead, they ask questions and listen carefully. They also don't lecture, threaten, or use sarcasm; rather, they work to construct solutions and find ways to bridge differences.

Be Unflailingly Honest. During a contentious conversation, don't portray yourself as the victim. Be sure to provide honest answers. If you don't have one or need more information, commit to getting the information that's requested and provide an honest timeline for your response.

Value and Use Data. Skillful leaders recognize the importance of data for decision-making. But they don't just cite statistics or repeat talking points. They place data in context and use it to illustrate their comments and suggestions. Understand that data often doesn't matter in emotional discussions. You probably won't persuade your critics with data. But anchor your response in solid data about the topic.

First, Always Focus on Students. Even though it's last on our list, the most important thing, regardless of the issue, or the behavior of the adults, is to always focus on doing what's best for students. That must always be at the forefront of any conversation with parents or community. It seems so obvious to always think about students first, but their interests are often secondary to the interests of other groups. While "what's best for students" is a term often used to support very divergent points of view, it is critical that leaders be able to explain and articulate the rationale for what they do, the policies they adopt, and the programs they support. Framing the issue around students and their needs is critical.

Assess Yourself

Area for Improvement	Steps I Can Take	How I Will Measure Improvement

Surround Teachers with Support

Teachers crave support, both tangible and intangible. Leaders must provide 360 support—assessing the needs that teachers, as a group, need, as well as those needed by individuals. When support is fragmented, teacher needs are not fully met, and they are not as motivated or effective as they could be.

The dilemma for a leader is that almost every staff member will seek support, but the definition of "support" will vary from person to person. Not everyone has the same needs as we mentioned earlier in the chapter on growth and resilience.

Support is not always about supplies and materials or dealing with a complicated parent issue. It's often the sense of both physical and emotional safety. A teacher wants to be safe in their school and classroom, be supported when trying new curricular and instructional strategies, and trusted to make critical instructional decisions that support student success.

Let's look at five areas that help us support teachers.

> Understand their needs.
> Pay attention to the unsaid.
> Prioritize what matters.
> Oblige when you can.
> Time matters.

Understand the Needs

In order to provide support, we need to understand what teachers actually need. It's easy to assume we know what a teacher wants. For example, in one school we worked with, the principal needed someone willing to take on an extra duty. He assumed no one would want to, and after receiving several turndowns, he stopped asking. A week later, a teacher came to him and offered to take the duty if he would work with her to leave after students were dismissed when her children had doctors' appointments. He was happy to oblige.

It's not enough to simply ask teachers what they need; we need to probe into different areas to be sure we understand the full issue. For example, Barbara worked with a district in Texas where teachers were required to participate in 20 hours of professional development. The leadership team surveyed, then interviewed focus groups of teachers to figure out how to schedule the training. What emerged were several clear obstacles to a schedule everyone could support. After gathering data, they worked with their leadership team to design a plan that worked for teachers.

> 1. Meetings would be held from 4:00 to 7:00 p.m. once a month.
> 2. Supervised childcare would be provided in an adjacent room.
> 3. High school family and consumer sciences students would provide a meal, paid for by the school.
> 4. Teachers could leave to pick up their children, or driver's education teachers would provide transportation for teachers' children if needed.
> 5. Teachers would be able to swap their time for two professional workdays, as long as there were not required duties on the day of their choice.

The teachers overwhelmingly supported the plan, and the professional development was successful.

Guide for Needs-Based Discussion with Teachers

	Concern(s)/Issue(s)	Explanations/Examples
Instruction		
Curriculum		
Assessment		
Classroom management		
Collaboration with other teachers		
Parent partnerships		
Administrative duties		
Extra duties		
Personal issues		
Other		

Pay Attention to the Unsaid

There are times when what is unsaid is more important than what is said. In other words, there are times a teacher may not verbalize a need, perhaps because they are minimizing their need or because they worry about the reaction of their leader or colleagues. Earlier, we discussed the importance of authentic listening and probing deeper to help understand their feelings and needs. For example, we worked with a school in South Carolina focusing on literacy across the curriculum. The math teachers were quiet when asked how they would use a particular graphic organizer. They weren't resistant, just non-responsive. The principal was frustrated and asked Barbara to talk with the teachers. After an informal discussion with the group, she returned to share what she had learned with the principal. Apparently, there had been a recent school-wide focus on saving money, which included not making copies unless absolutely necessary. In fact, teachers were on a paper allotment. The graphic organizer we had recommended worked best when students were provided a copy. As one teacher said, "You told us what worked, but we can't do that and meet our paper allotment." The principal realized her resource mandate was negatively impacting instruction. She immediately told the teachers that she would run any copies of the graphic organizer out of her leadership allocation so they could implement the tool. The teachers were happy, students learned, and the problem was solved.

Prioritize What Matters

Often, leaders feel a need to make an immediate decision, respond to a request, or answer a question. It's easy to fall into that trap. But other times, what may be best is to take time to gather other perspectives, consider all the alternatives, and make a decision based on that thoughtful analysis.

Oblige When You Can

One key aspect of meeting needs is knowing what you can and what you cannot do. For example, one of your teachers may want to miss a meeting because their child is ill or has a medical appointment. You know it's better to have them work all day rather than take a sick day. But district policy is clear about the obligation for meetings. Understand how to balance needs and policy and when you can make exceptions. And if you can't, always be able to explain your reasons. Remember, "It's policy" or "That's the way we do things" isn't a good answer, because almost always people know of an exception that has been made.

Time Matters

In many ways, time is your best support tool. Time is the biggest challenge for many teachers. Time management, as well as balancing work and personal life, is always a challenge. We will discuss the importance of both in Chapter 10.

But a major issue related to time is the school schedule. Often, one year's schedule looks like the previous year. When that occurs, it means that some grades, or subjects, get the same advantages, or disadvantages, from the schedule.

The structure of the school day can impact both morale and motivation. Teachers want a schedule that meets their instruction needs. At the elementary level, that might be long uninterrupted instructional blocks, preferably in the morning. At middle and high school, it may be a schedule that avoids sharing rooms or that provides breaks throughout the day.

Ways to Provide Collaborative Time	
Common planning	When teachers share a common planning period, some of the time may be used for collaborative work.
Parallel scheduling	When special teachers (physical education, music, art, etc.) are scheduled so that grade-level or content-area teachers have common planning.
Shared classes	Teachers in more than one grade or team combine their students into a single large class for specific instruction, and the other teachers can collaborate.
Faculty meeting	Find other ways to communicate the routine items shared during faculty meetings, and reallocate that time to collaborative activities.
Adjust start or end of day	Members of a team, grade, or entire school agree to start their workday early or extend their workday one day a week to gain collaborative time.
Late start or early release	Adjust the start or end of the school day for students and use the time for collaborative activity.
Professional development days	Rather than traditional large group professional development, use the time for teams of teachers to engage in collaborative work.

Source: Adapted from Williamson (2009), DuFour, DuFour, Eaker, and Many (2006).

Regardless of the need, the first step is to start a conversation about the schedule with stakeholder. Work to establish clear goals for the schedule. Value the collaboration, the conversation. Listen intently for needs. Assure a balanced review, and commit to varying the schedule from year to year so that any negative impacts don't affect the same teachers every year.

Final Thoughts

Words matter, and the choice of words matters when dealing with both parents and teachers and other employees. The most effective leaders recognize the impact of their words and choose them carefully. They recognize that terms like "support" are used in different ways to label different needs. They also understand the importance of creating processes that allow for open, candid conversation among constituent groups, processes that focus on skillful listening and thoughtful action.

5

Hiring and Retaining Faculty

> Motivation Connection:
> You want to hire and retain quality faculty. In addition to other characteristics, consider how to address their intrinsic motivation: value (relevance, autonomy, and relationships) and success.

One of a principal's major responsibilities is hiring and supervision of employees. Virtually all school districts have policies and procedures on both hiring and evaluation. Although those requirements vary, the process is often similar.

We're not going to focus on the legal requirements—those vary from state to state. Instead, we'll focus on how school leaders can use the hiring process, and the supervision and evaluation process, to motivate, nurture, and retain quality employees.

Finding the Right People

When hiring, the use of a standard process ensures that you will treat everyone who applies in a uniform manner. Your district may have some of these procedures in place. If not, you will need to create them for your school.

First, develop your selection criteria. Each criterion should be relevant to the work to be performed and should be free of bias, so that everyone is treated the same throughout the process. If you need someone who is bilingual, include that on your list. However, as you plan, differentiate between those skills or characteristics that are required and those that are simply desirable. All criteria must be relevant to the work, but you are likely to have some nonnegotiable items and some that you would like to have in a candidate.

Remember that even a job description sends subtle messages about the climate and culture of your school and your vision for student success.

Next, create and use a protocol for interviews. The questions should be linked to your selection criteria, and they should be open-ended, so as to provide in-depth information about the candidate.

We've learned from principals that the questions you ask can tell a candidate something about your school, your priorities, and your values. The candidate's response will tell you about how they react to those priorities and values.

Think about the questions you might ask that would align with the things valued by the new generation of teachers. You might consider questions such as, "What do you see as your strengths related to this position?" "What leadership skills do you bring that could be immediately used to improve our school?" "Imagine you were offered the position and accepted it and it is one year later. What was the best part of your first year, and what was your biggest challenge?"

Listen attentively to the candidate's response, but also look for non-verbal clues in body language, eyes, and facial expressions. They will tell you a lot about the candidate.

Using open-ended questions allows the candidate to talk and provides an opportunity for you, and your hiring committee, to gather information about the candidates. As with most things, a little courtesy goes a long way. Make sure the candidate is comfortable. Introduce everyone in the room. Don't cut off a candidate's answers. Avoid reacting to anything they say. Always thank them for considering your school and district, and provide a timeline for a decision.

Many teacher candidates are looking at positions in multiple districts. They often have a choice about where they work. Often, the interview is as much an interview of you and your school community as it is of the candidate. Use the interview

> Take Action: What is a specific question or type of question you want to include in your interviews?

as an opportunity to make a good impression with the candidate, and assure that your school ends up as their first choice.

New Generations of Teachers

Baby boomer teachers, who dominated American society for a generation, are rapidly retiring and being replaced by younger teachers, members of new generations, referred to as Generation Y, Generation Z, or millennials. They hold very different beliefs about work and about the workplace and the way principals work with them (Coggins, 2008).

While inappropriate to generalize about these generations, what is clear is that they were raised, and educated, in a society far different than those of earlier generations. Their life experiences shape their beliefs and values and their approach to work. They watched older generations struggle with the balance between work and personal lives. They are very aware of social inequity in our society, and they are far more comfortable with technology than their predecessors are.

Characteristics of New Generations

- Highly educated, value education, and attribute their success to education.
- Very comfortable using technology and expect it to be available in the workplace.
- Tend to be creative, innovative, and self-confident.
- Committed to making a difference and contributing to positive social change.
- Want to be connected, updated, and included and involved in their work.
- Desire relationships with coworkers and supervisors.
- Looking for immediate opportunities for growth, challenging work and assignments, and flexibility in work schedules.
- Possess collaborative skills, are committed to team-building, and are not afraid of accountability.

There are several strategies that leaders can use to work well with these new generation of teachers.

- *Establish shared vision and goals.* They want to be involved and participate in setting a vision and identifying specific, measurable goals. They value social responsibility and recognize education as a path to address inequities in society.
- *Provide leadership opportunities.* They expect to be involved and to assume responsibility. They will not simply defer to more senior teachers.
- *Create a positive, supportive school culture.* Celebrate generational diversity and use cross-generational teams to work on curricular and instructional issues.
- *Provide professional development.* An opportunity to continue to learn is important to this group. It improves their job satisfaction and the likelihood of staying at your school.
- *Provide sound instructional leadership.* They expect in-depth feedback because they want to contribute to the success of your school and expect to receive honest, open, and personalized support from you. They particularly value coaching and mentorship.
- *Embrace technology.* This generation is comfortable using technology and will expect to use all forms of technology to improve their work.
- *Use data effectively and often.* This generation of teachers is comfortable with accountability and the use of data. They appreciate access to user-friendly data that can be used to improve their work.

Source: Adapted from Behrstock and Clifford (2009), Gomez, Mawhinney, and Betts (2020), and Rogers (2021).

Onboarding New Teachers

Hiring a new teacher is only the start. In order to keep a new hire motivated, you'll need to consider how to onboard your teachers. For principals, it is how to welcome and support new teachers or teachers new to your school.

Almost every school district has a formal onboarding process. But the most important "onboarding" occurs at the school level, when a new teacher arrives on campus and becomes part of your school community. New teachers often want to visit their physical classroom and meet formally, or informally, with grade or content colleagues. They may be unfamiliar with the formal, and informal, norms and operations of the school.

So what do you do? We've identified some of the best advice from principals and other leaders who welcomed new teachers while working remotely.

- ♦ **Establish Personal Connections to Activate the Value Aspect of Motivation.** Often, a new employee is shown around the school and introduced to other teachers, or they might be introduced in a staff meeting. Leverage virtual meeting tools to introduce new teachers. In Chapter 3, we shared an example of a principal who invited every new teacher as well as the veterans to create a short video introduction.
- ♦ **Assign a Mentor or Coach to Help Them Be Successful.** Identify another staff member or a grade/content team to assist the new teacher in learning the curriculum and/or locating instructional resources.
- ♦ **Assure IT Support to Help Them Be Successful.** Most new hires have experience with technology, but they may not be familiar with the systems used at your school. Make sure the teacher knows how to contact IT for needed support. You might ask your school's IT contact to proactively reach out and ask the teacher how they can be of assistance. Since many schools may occasionally revert to remote learning due to weather emergencies or other school closures, make sure new teachers are familiar with the remote learning model.
- ♦ **Celebrations and Recognitions.** Be attentive to scheduling of events, like recognition of birthdays or other

celebrations, so that the new teacher is included in those events.
- **Encourage Wellness to Meet Their Needs.** Schools, and schooling, have become far more politicized in recent years. Controversy over health mandates, curriculum, and school safety has shaped the work of most educators. It's been a struggle for many teachers and other staff. This uncertainty raised anxiety and disrupted established routines in both their personal and professional lives. Many districts have mindfulness and wellness resources for their staff. Assure that your new teachers know about these resources, and encourage their use when appropriate.
- **How to Get Help to Ensure Success.** Make sure new teachers know how to get help if needed. Let them know how to contact you, or others in your office, if they have questions or need assistance.

Take Action: Which of these strategies would help you onboard teachers?

Retaining Good Employees

Whether you have hired your own staff or inherited them from a former administrator, you want to keep the right people. Schools are basically people places, so it is important to nurture and cultivate talented employees and make them feel valued and part of the organization.

Steps to Create a "People-Oriented" Workplace

- See each person as an individual, as unique.
- Provide opportunities for each individual to assume responsibility.
- Remind individuals about the need for strict compliance with rules, but consider exceptions when appropriate.
- Create a place where people seek to learn from the experience, and consider other alternatives rather than lay blame when things don't work out.

- Value listening and respecting varied points of view.
- Allow flexibility for people to teach or organize their classrooms in different ways.
- Provide opportunities for leadership to everyone.

As a leader, you must recognize three things that have been shown to improve employee satisfaction, motivation, and morale: effective communication, engagement in significant tasks, and valuing and respecting different points of view.

Effective Communication

Your first key to employee satisfaction is your ability to communicate effectively with your employees. When communicating, focus more energy on listening than speaking. Remember that much communication occurs through body language, so be attentive to nonverbal cues about meaning. Be aware of any power relationship (supervisor–supervisee, evaluator–evaluatee) that may be influencing the situation. Throughout the conversation, ask clarifying questions and probe for deeper meaning in response to any comments. Overall, focus on mutual problem-solving and look for win–win solutions. And always identify next steps for each person, which will clarify each person's responsibilities.

Engagement in Significant Tasks

Next, quality employees are more likely to be satisfied if they are engaged in significant tasks. Identify meaningful ways to involve employees in school decision-making rather than involving them in trivial decisions, such as the location of a copier. For all tasks, be clear in defining the task, the desired or required timeline, and any resources that will be provided. Earlier in the chapter we discussed the new generation of teachers and the characteristics they look for in the workplace.

Valuing and Respecting Different Points of View

Another key to retaining employees is your choice to respect points of view that differ from your own. Make it clear that you value freedom of expression, and reinforce that in every aspect of your job. When hearing unpleasant news, rather than reacting defensively, be open and probe for understanding by asking clarifying questions. Structure meetings and other activities to model openness, and use a decision-making process that requires exploration of alternatives and an analysis of advantages and disadvantages. Activities such as these will reinforce for your employees that you are open to differing perspectives.

Assess Yourself

Element	I'm Okay but Need to Work on This Area	I Think I Do a Satisfactory Job	I Go Over and Above in This Area	Evidence for Your Assessment
Effective communication				
Engagement in significant tasks				
Valuing and respecting different points of view				

Coaching, Not Evaluating

Teachers value, and respond well to, coaching and other opportunities to reflect on their own teaching. This collaborative approach engages teachers but, at the same time, doesn't reward less-skillful teaching. Teachers value the chance to work with their principal and/or other teachers to analyze their instruction and develop plans for strengthening their practice. Similarly, teachers crave feedback and an opportunity to reflect on their work. Rather than resisting supervision, they seek authentic, risk-free opportunities to talk about their teaching and to grow professionally.

We're not minimizing the evaluation process. It's a requirement in every state and something that must be done. We suggest that conversations that occur during the formal evaluation process can also follow a collaborative coaching model. But we also know that there are times, with some employees, when a much more direct approach is needed.

Become a Powerful Coach

The principal, rather than being the expert and telling a teacher what to do, serves as the "lead coach" responsible for engaging teachers in a process that respects them as learners and works with them to reflect on their teaching and identify ways to strengthen their practice. When principals serve as coaches, it is critical that the two roles remain separate and that clear boundaries be established about how information from coaching will be used. The evidence shows that teachers are able to separate the roles.

The primary role of the coach is to ask questions that are open-ended and promote cognition. Listening, probing for deeper meaning, and being nonjudgmental are critical skills. Good coaching is built on a foundation of trust. It occurs when the coach creates an open, respectful, and inviting setting. Coaching cannot be forced. Good coaches share several traits. They:

- **Enroll Teachers**. Coaching cannot be seen as punishment or as a requirement. Good coaches create a setting that welcomes teachers and in which teachers choose to participate.
- **Identify Teacher Goals**. A top-down approach rarely works. Good coaches help teachers identify goals for their work and support teachers' efforts to improve.
- **Listen**. Perhaps no other skill is as important as the ability to listen intently to those being coached. Good coaches create a setting where teachers feel comfortable, can be candid without fear of retribution, and are curious and inquisitive.
- **Ask Thoughtful Questions**. Good coaches ask thoughtful, open-ended questions that promote reflection. They are interested in promoting teacher cognition rather than providing answers. You might also use appropriate prompts.

> Acknowledgment prompts include "Tell me more," "I understand," or "I'm following you."
>
> Reflective prompts you might use are "So you would like ... " "I think you're saying ... " or "You feel ... because ... ."

Provide Feedback. Good coaches don't provide feedback in the traditional sense. They don't tell teachers what to do. But they are comfortable using data from an observation, or comments made by the teacher, to provide feedback. All feedback is precise and nonjudgmental. Good coaches are always open to the teacher's point of view (Garmston & Wellman, 2013; Hirsh & Killion, 2007).

Finally, there are specific conditions that can assist in being a good coach.

Conditions for Successful Coaching

The conditions that support effective coaching include:

- Presume positive intentions.
- Talk with the teacher to identify a focus for the coaching. Assume the teacher can analyze and reflect on their teaching and identify an area for growth.
- Ask clarifying questions to understand the context (students, content, prior learning), the lesson, and the teacher's thinking about the design and delivery of the lesson.
- Remain nonjudgmental.
- Listen attentively and authentically; use paraphrasing to indicate that you are listening and understand what was said.

A Coaching Model

Every year, principals are expected to formally evaluate many of the teachers in their school. While some teachers may be formally evaluated, the principal should be supervising all teaching staff. Sally Zepeda described this work as "the most important work a supervisor does" (2012). The key to retaining a quality staff is to engage all teachers in a process in which they reflect on their teaching, collaborate with others, and grow professionally.

Three-Step Model

One of the most prominent models for promoting teacher growth was called the clinical supervision model. Most teacher evaluation systems incorporate some variation of the approach. But it is a powerful model, when used outside of evaluation, to engage teachers in reflection on their teaching, a formative process.

The model is built around three components—a planning or pre-observation conference, observation, and a post-observation conference. The approach includes three phases: planning, observation, and analysis and reflection.

While often used by school leaders, this model can also be used by peers, or curriculum specialists, to engage teachers in examining their own teaching practices. The focus is on learning, reinforcing things that go well, and developing strategies to modify things that may not go as well. It is not a judgmental or evaluative model.

Step 1: Planning or Pre-Observation Conference

During this step, the teacher and colleague or school leader meet to discuss the lesson being taught during the observation. It also provides an opportunity for the teacher to share any contextual information about prior instruction or about students in the class.

Conditions for Success

- Meet at a mutually agreed-upon time and in a mutually agreed-upon location.
- Presume positive intentions.
- Ask clarifying questions in order to understand the context (students, prior lessons, where this lesson fits into the curriculum) and the planned lesson.

- ♦ Arrange seating around a table or in a way that promotes conversation; avoid sitting behind your desk.
- ♦ Avoid distractions—no texts, calls, or emails.
- ♦ Listen attentively and authentically.

Most important, the planning conference should include a conversation to identify the focus of the observation. Central to the model is the premise that the teacher can analyze and reflect on his or her own teaching. Part of that reflection is to identify the focus of the observation and to identify a tool the administrator will use to collect data about the lesson.

Discussion Prompts

- ♦ "Thank you for meeting with me today to talk about the upcoming visit to your class. In order to plan for that visit, I would like to talk with you about your students, the lesson you plan, and the ways in which I may be of help to you during the observation."
- ♦ "I always enjoy the opportunity to visit classrooms. What sort of data can I collect during my visit that would be helpful to you?"
- ♦ "Tell me about your students. What is important for me to know about them? Their learning?"
- ♦ "Talk with me about the curriculum for your class. What skills have you been working on? How is this lesson connected to prior learning?"

For example, one elementary teacher wanted data about the distribution of response opportunities among her students. Her colleague agreed to use a seating chart of the room to chart the number of times that the teacher called on or interacted with each student throughout the lesson. The result was a visual map of teacher–student interactions during the observation.

> **Key Steps of the Pre-Observation Conference**
>
> - Decide the focus of the observation.
> - Determine the method and form of observation.
> - Agree upon the time of the observation and post-observation conference.

Step 2: Observation

Throughout the observation, the observer gathers data about the focus area agreed to during the planning conference. You should be clear about the tool to be used to gather data. Your goal is for the teacher to be comfortable with the instrument used during the visit. Ideally, you have shared the form or tool with the teacher in advance of the observation. At the end of the observation, verify the meeting time and location for the post-observation conference, begin to analyze the data, and think about the questions that you will use during the conference to elicit teacher reflection and thinking about their lesson.

> **Key Steps of the Observation**
>
> - Conduct the observation.
> - Verify the post-observation conference time, and offer the teacher a copy of the data.
> - Analyze the facts of the observation.
> - Choose an approach to use during the post-observation conference.

Step 3: Post-Observation Conference

The post-observation conference provides an opportunity for the administrator to meet with the teacher and have a conversation about the observation.

Conditions for Success

- Meet at a mutually agreed-upon time and in a mutually agreed-upon location.
- Presume positive intentions.
- Ask clarifying questions in order to understand the lesson and the teacher's thinking about both the design and the delivery of the lesson.
- Summarize and identify appropriate next steps.
- Arrange seating around a table or in a way that promotes conversation; avoid sitting behind your desk.
- Avoid distractions—no texts, calls, or emails.
- Listen attentively and authentically; use paraphrasing to indicate that you are listening and understand what has been said.

This should provide an opportunity for the teacher to reflect on the data collected in the focus area and for the teacher to analyze and think about his or her teaching. The meeting should conclude with agreement on a plan to follow up and the appropriate next steps.

Discussion Prompts

- "Thank you for meeting with me today. I would like to spend some time talking with you about the lesson."
- "Let's talk about your planning. When you plan a lesson, what are the things that you consider in its design?"
- "What strategies do you use to ensure that each lesson is linked to students' prior learning?"
- "Describe for me the ways you monitor whether or not your students are learning what you are teaching."
- "Talk me through the process you use to plan a lesson. What do you consider? How do you proceed?"
- "Occasionally, I'm in the middle of a lesson and I know it is not working the way I would like. When that happens

- to you, how do you adjust your teaching? What data/information do you use to guide adjustments?"
- "When you teach this lesson again, what adjustments might you make in its design?"
- "Talk with me about the strengths of this lesson. What would you describe as its strengths? What evidence do you have to support these strengths?"
- "Let's spend a few minutes analyzing this lesson. How do you critique the lesson and its implementation?"
- "Let's think about next steps. What additional support can I provide for you and your teaching? What data can I collect? During my next visit, on what area of instruction would you like me to focus?"
- Note: This process should appropriately be modified for a less-experienced teacher or one with performance concerns.

It is easy to shortcut this aspect of the process, particularly with stronger teachers, but it is a critical part of the reflective process, has an impact on teacher motivation, and should receive its due attention. Often your most-skilled teachers are most interested in an opportunity to reflect on their teaching and consider ways to continue to grow professionally.

Key Steps of the Post-Observation Conference

- Share the data and elicit the teacher's thinking about the lesson.
- Reflect on the teacher's comments so that you are clear on his or her thinking.
- Begin to think together about ways to refine the lesson. Focus on the things that should be affirmed and continued as well as things that might be modified.
- Engage in a discussion of the ideas and options.
- Agree on a plan and follow-up.

Final Thoughts

Hiring and retaining a quality staff is a leader's most important role. We've found that the processes you use to hire, onboard, and supervise teachers, and other staff, send powerful messages about your school and your leadership and impact motivation. Teachers choose to work in places where they are valued and where there are clear opportunities for growth.

6

What's Trust Got to Do with It?

> Motivation Connection: If teachers don't trust leaders, there is no authenticity. It can destroy the relationship aspect of value.

> Reflection Point: How do you define trust?

Every time Ron taught a course about the principalship, he started the semester by asking students to describe a good school leader, the sort of person teachers and others would want to lead their school. Every semester the same response topped the list. They wanted a leader they could trust.

Students were then asked to describe "trust" and what behaviors a leader who is "trustworthy" displays. Again and again, year after year, the same characteristics were identified. They wanted a leader who made them feel safe, valued, who challenged them but at the same time supported their creativity and advocated for the resource to support their success. They wanted a leader who was loyal to their school, and the staff, and whose first priority were students and staff. And they wanted a leader who respected them as professionals, valued their insights, and was committed to a collaborative work setting.

> **Importance of Trustworthy Leadership**
>
> ♦ Physical and emotional safety
> ♦ Loyalty to employees and the organization
> ♦ Commitment to collaboration

A study published in *Harvard Business Review* (Zenger & Folkman, 2019) of characteristics that serve as the foundation for trust found similar things. The researchers identified three categories—positive relationships, good judgment and expertise, and consistency.

Why Trust Is Important

Researchers found that a high level of trust is "highly correlated with how people rate a leader's overall leadership effectiveness" (Zenger & Folkman, 2019, p. 3). They also identified three elements of trust that contribute to a leader being seen as "trustworthy" (Zenger & Folkman, 2019).

> Positive Relationships. The first element is a measure of "the extent to which a leader is able to create positive relationships with people and groups." For school leaders, that may include getting to know individual teachers and other employees, working to resolve conflict and generate cooperation, and expressing concern for others.
>
> Good Judgment and Expertise. A second component of trust is "the extent to which a leader is well-informed and knowledgeable." This includes an understanding of the technical side of the work as well as experience. In schools, that might include a measure of the leader's understanding of curriculum and instruction, of school–community relations, and student discipline and management.
>
> Consistency. The third element of trust is "the extent to which leaders walk their talk and do what they say they will do."

In other words, leaders must honor commitments and model behaviors they expect from others.

Assess Yourself

Element	I'm Okay but Need to Work on This Area	I Think I Do a Satisfactory Job	I Go Over and Above in This Area	Evidence for Your Assessment
Positive relationships				
Good judgment and expertise				
Consistency				

When leaders display these attributes, their employees are more likely to describe them as trustworthy. But of the three, it was found that building and sustaining positive relationships mattered the most when building trust. In part, employees need to feel valued by their leaders.

The next section describes ten behaviors that build and sustain trust, including nurturing and sustaining positive relationships.

Furthermore, when trust is present, people are generally more productive, are more satisfied with their jobs, put in greater discretionary effort, and are less likely to search for new jobs (Zak, 2019).

Similarly, when trust is present in a school, employees see it as a desirable place to work, and parents see it as a desirable place to educate their children. It's a place where employees are more likely to remain even during times of stress, and it's the sort of setting where people are more committed to working collaboratively on behalf of students and their learning.

Reflection Point: In what ways do you build trust with your faculty and staff?

Ten Behaviors to Build and Sustain Trust

Trust is recognized as an essential attribute of successful leaders, but it's also a rather amorphous term that always takes on the context of the employee and the employer. Fortunately, there is a set of leadership behaviors that, when present, build, nurture, and sustain trust (Miller, 2022).

What a leader does, what they say, and how they spend their time send signals about what is important. Leaders must model trust if they want to be seen as trustworthy.

Here are ten behaviors that leaders can adopt to build, nurture, and sustain trust. Adopting each of these behaviors models leadership that others will emulate and use in their own work.

Leadership Behaviors That Build Trust

- Follow through on commitments
- Admit mistakes and correct them quickly
- Build positive relationships
- Avoid being judgmental
- Show gratitude
- Demonstrate vulnerability
- Maintain confidentiality
- Hold clear expectations
- Manage change
- Act with confidence

Follow Through on Commitments. One thing employees value is predictability, and one of the best ways to demonstrate predictability is to always keep your word and follow through on things you commit to do. Always commit to things that you know you can do, and if you can't, explain why. Teachers and other employees value the security of predictability, and to sustain trust, a leader must always deliver on promises and commitments. Avoid using consistency as a substitute for predictability. There are times when consistency is inappropriate and a new approach is needed. When that occurs, be open about your rationale, but be "predictable" about how you follow through on issues.

Examples of Following Through on Commitments

Set and meet deadlines for tasks and projects.
Respond to emails in a regularly consistent manner.

Admit Mistakes and Correct Them Quickly. A companion to predictability is admitting when things don't work. Every leader understands that not everything works as planned. Openly acknowledging when that occurs, or when you made an inappropriate decision, and working to amend your decision is essential to building and sustaining trust. Owning one's mistakes acknowledges accountability by the leader. It also acknowledges that failure is part of life, and minimizes any sense among employees that they must always be perfect. You want your teachers, and other employees, to also acknowledge when things don't work, and to be creative in developing for another strategy.

Sample Statements

"I made a mistake. This is how I'm addressing it, and this is how I am ensuring it won't happen again."

"I realize that what I planned didn't work. What I want to do is listen to your feedback and, together, create a new plan."

Build Positive Relationships. An essential component of trust is the presence of positive relationships between the leader and others. In fact, as mentioned earlier, there's evidence that it may be the most important component. A leader must always stay in touch with others and demonstrate a concern for others. They must work to create a climate of cooperation among employees, work to minimize conflict with others, and always provide feedback in a helpful way. Always recognize how your words, actions, and behavior affect others. Identify any emotional triggers you hold, and develop a process for working through them. Be open to receiving feedback, and ask clarifying questions to fully understand that feedback. And always practice good listening skills, skills that demonstrate authentic listening.

Ten Tips for Listening

1. Make eye contact.
2. Use positive body language.
3. Restate or affirm what the other person is saying.
4. Ask clarifying questions to help you understand the information.
5. Wait to share your comment until the other person is finished.
6. Pause and allow silence if appropriate.
7. Be fully present and avoid distractions.
8. Keep an open mind.
9. React to the content, not the person. Never personalize the issue.
10. If you choose to take notes, inform the other person and explain why. That way, they don't think you are ignoring them.

Avoid Being Judgmental. Nothing suppresses motivation faster than judgmental behavior from the leader. It makes employees feel insecure, and they are less likely to be creative and innovative. Recognize how both your verbal and non-verbal behavior can signal judgment, and be intentional in how you respond to a question, a problem, or feedback you receive. Always be open to talking with employees. Ask questions for clarification and deeper understanding.

Don't Let Assumptions Make You Judgmental

Assumptions can also undermine your ability to listen and, therefore, communicate. You might assume you already know what a person thinks or how they feel, assuming they have the same background knowledge that you do or believing they should interpret that knowledge the same way you do.

Show Gratitude. Always express gratitude for the work people do. Remind people how important their work is to your school's mission and vision. Assure that everyone is acknowledged, not just the most successful or the most innovative. Be genuinely appreciative of individuals' work by offering specific comments that let them know you are aware of what they do and how they contribute to your school's success. Minimize general comments that apply to everyone so that each individual feels your gratitude and appreciation.

Ways to Show Gratitude

"Paws of Praise" notes.
Provide snacks or dessert for teachers.
Positive "shout-outs" in newsletters or on social media.

Demonstrate Vulnerability. Vulnerability can be uncomfortable, particularly when it involves risk or emotional exposure. But demonstrating vulnerability is also important to building trust. School leaders must be willing to engage in tough conversations, to focus on solving difficult and challenging problems, acknowledging that it's time for a new or different perspective, and modeling how to move on from a setback or failure (Brown, 2018). Leaders must be willing to gather feedback about their leadership, share the results, and discuss ways to strengthen and improve their work. As with the other behaviors, modeling vulnerability communicates to your employees that it's also important for them to adopt this skill.

> **Examples of Vulnerable Behavior**
>
> Admitting and/or owning a mistake.
> Sharing lessons learned from your past.

Maintain Confidentiality. One of the fastest ways to lose trust is to share confidential, sensitive, or personal information shared with you in the workplace. If confidentiality is not maintained, it undermines employee morale and leads people to not be open and candid when you need them to be. This behavior is one of the keys to assuring emotional safety for your teachers and other employees.

> **Ways to Ensure Confidentiality**
>
> Be careful whom you talk with.
> If you have a conversation about sensitive information, be sure all parties are clear and committed to confidentiality.
> Understand emails are probably subject to freedom of information requests if you are a public school and, therefore, are not confidential.

Hold Clear Expectations. Also linked to predictability is the importance of having clear expectations for your employees and others in your school community. Employees want to know what is expected of them, and they want their leader to monitor what is done. Talk with employees about expectations, assure reasonable timelines for their work, and always be open to modifying them as needed. Some of the most successful school leaders work collaboratively with teachers, and others, to set those expectations. That assures they are reasonable and attainable.

> **Sample Clear Expectations**
>
> Instead of "Do your job," design engaging lessons, select materials that motivate all learners, respond to parent calls within 24 hours, and be in your classroom to greet students.

Manage Change. Every school deals with change. Often, it occurs in subtle ways over the school year, but occasionally, it is more dramatic and impactful. Successful leaders help their school community deal with change. That includes providing the information and resources to support the change, gathering appropriate input into decisions that must be made, and monitoring and adjusting the plans as needed. Most people don't resist change just to resist; rather, they desire information about what is changing, including a compelling rationale for the change, an opportunity for professional development to support the change, and the resources to assure success in implementing the change.

> Help stakeholders adapt to change.
> Provide time, information, professional development, and resources.

Act with Confidence. Successful school leaders hold a clear vision for their school and act in ways that demonstrate their belief in the vision and its impact on their school community. Leaders must be willing to expand their knowledge, including talking with people who may not agree or support their vision. They must always express confidence in their beliefs but also recognize areas where they must continue to grow as a leader. Confident leaders understand that they may not have strengths in all areas, and they develop a cadre of people they can work with to complement their strengths.

How to Demonstrate Confidence

Dress to reflect your confidence.
Watch your body language.
Use firm but not aggressive words.
Back up your confidence with research, data, and information.

Final Thoughts

Building and sustaining trust is not easy. It requires hard work, and at times, it may feel overwhelming and uncomfortable. But the absence of trust almost always undermines a leader's success.

A collaborative school community is a natural extension of a school where trust is present. Collaboration improves decisions, empowers teachers and other employees, and allows all stakeholders to develop ownership for continuous improvement. In the next chapter, we'll look at collaboration to build ownership and provide tools and strategies for nurturing a collaborative school.

7

Empowerment and Ownership

> Motivation Connection: Empowering teachers helps them feel successful; empowerment and ownership also build value.

For decades, it's been suggested that leaders build ownership and empower employees. The problem is that the terms have been so overused and inappropriately used that they have become almost meaningless.

But don't discount the importance of creating ownership and empowering your teachers and other employees. There are clear links between the presence of those two things, adult motivation, and a successful school.

This chapter won't spend much time reviewing the research. What it will do is provide a working definition of both concepts, discuss how they are both linked to trust and motivation, and provide concrete steps for making your school a place where teachers and other staff feel ownership and are empowered to do their best to assure that every student succeeds.

Authenticity

In too many schools, *ownership* and *empowerment* are used to describe all sorts of collaborative activity. Many schools form school improvement teams, or leadership teams, because they are required by state law or local policy rather than a real desire to build ownership and empower teachers. And occasionally, the decisions those teams are asked to make deal with operational and logistical issues, like scheduling assemblies or access to copiers, rather than substantive issues about curriculum, instruction, or student safety.

Reflection Point: How do we currently provide ownership and empowerment opportunities for teachers?

When building ownership, it's important to be authentic, to be true to yourself. Authenticity means you know, and are true, to your own values and beliefs, and you resist pressure to act otherwise. When you're authentic, you're honest with yourself, and others; you take responsibility for your actions, including your mistakes. In other words, your action aligns with your values and beliefs. So others see you as genuine and trustworthy. Trustworthiness means others will connect with you, building the value aspect of motivation.

Authenticity is an important trait of a leader, particularly when working in an environment that expects collaboration and values diverse points of view. Being authentic means you trust yourself to do the right thing.

It's not always easy to be an authentic leader. Your supervisor, or others in the organization, may push you to act in ways that aren't aligned with your values and beliefs. The role may imply expectations about action, and behavior, that don't fit your concept of the role. Acting in ways that aren't aligned with your own values and beliefs is often apparent to those you work with and undermines trust and respect they have in you and your decisions.

Benefits to Being Authentic

- *Trust and Respect.* When you act in authentic ways, you are true to your own values. Therefore, you trust your actions, and others will trust you as well.
- *Integrity.* An authentic leader also has integrity. They don't hesitate to do the right thing and, thus, don't have to second-guess their decisions and actions.

- *Ability to Deal with Problems.* When you're authentic, you are able to deal with problems quickly because you know your values and beliefs. There's no need to procrastinate or ignore the need to act.
- *Confidence and Self-Esteem.* The authentic leader trusts themselves to make the right decision. This leads to greater confidence and self-esteem and greater satisfaction with one's judgment.
- *Less Stress.* Finally, being authentic is less stressful for a leader. You're not worried about what others think, or whether you made the right decision. Self-confidence lessens the stress of decision-making.

(Mind Tools, 2023)

Becoming Authentic

Every leader recognizes the pressure to adopt certain behaviors or act in certain ways. Once you become a "principal," both teachers and parents may expect that you conform to their expectations for the job. Similarly, you may feel pressure from your supervisor to conform to their norms for the job.

So how does a leader develop authenticity? How do you align your action, your decisions, your judgment with your authentic self?

1. *Identify your values and live by them.* In an earlier chapter, we discussed the importance of vision, both your personal vision and the collective vision for your school. A critical step in developing one's personal vision is to be clear about the values and beliefs they hold that are central to their life, to their being. If you've not done so, spend time thinking about those beliefs. Which are unalienable? Which are so sacrosanct that they can never be set aside?
2. *Identify gaps between values and action.* Think about your action during the past week, and identify gaps between your stated values and the decisions you made. Prepare a list of words to

describe actions that align with your values. Then select one to focus on during the next week. Begin the work to align values and action.
3. *Communicate honestly.* Good communication skills are essential for every leader. Regardless of the skills or your personal style of communicating, it's essential that you say what you mean and are honest when interacting with others. That doesn't mean you're brutally honest, saying anything that comes to mind. You can be truthful and tactful, respecting other's feelings and needs.
4. *Assure integrity.* We often intuitively know when a decision we made was sound or when it might have been better. Unease about an action often signals that there were other alternatives. When one has integrity, they take responsibility for their actions, including things that didn't work. They are open about shortcomings and work to correct them.
5. *Avoid making assumptions.* Rather than making assumptions about others, authentic leaders let others' actions speak for themselves. When you avoid making assumptions, it is often reciprocated by others.
6. *Develop self-confidence and manage emotions.* An authentic leader is confident in their actions because they are clear that actions align with values and beliefs. Their self-confidence helps them persevere when others challenge their judgment. And when challenged, an authentic leader always treats people with courtesy and respect. They respect other points of view, but confidence in their beliefs helps them remain steadfast.

Creating a School Where Employees Feel Empowered

Empowerment is described as the level of influence and control people have over things in their lives. Empowerment allows you to take initiative, make decisions for yourself, and address complex problems. For teachers, and other school employees, it's about the extent to which they feel they have control, or autonomy, to make decisions and take action, based on their professional judgment. Each of these factors impacts motivation.

Obviously, every employee doesn't have absolute freedom to do whatever they want, but an empowered employee will feel that they have autonomy to act based on the agreed-upon vision and mission and other parameters from collaborative decision-making. There's an implicit shifting of power to the teacher rather than relying on the principal for direction.

But you want employees who feel that they are enabled to represent their interests, the interests of students, and the community and who feel safe challenging the status quo or working to develop alternatives.

What Works to Create Empowerment

There are six basic approaches to creating empowerment.

- Involve in planning and decisions.
- Provide professional development and support.
- Balance direction and support.
- Encourage autonomy.
- Communicate to build trust.
- Recognize employees.

Involve in Planning and Decisions. Building autonomy begins with involving teachers, and other employees, in planning and decision-making. That doesn't mean that they are involved in every little decision, but rather, they are involved in creating the vision for your school and provide input into how to achieve that vision. Taking time to create, or affirm, a vision with your staff improves motivation because it allows individuals to see how they can contribute and the value of their contribution.

Involvement is also a way to foster collaboration. It models how you work with others and use that collaborative time for both your own learning and expand the ideas and experiences they have to improve their contributions to your school.

Provide Professional Development and Support. Along with involvement, it is also important to provide opportunities to learn and to demonstrate one's skills. Support continued professional development for your teachers, including the opportunity to learn from one another. Make sure that when individuals participate in professional learning or attend conferences, they share what they've learned with others on your staff.

Balance Direction and Support. It's important to be clear about expectations and boundaries for work. Employees appreciate clarity about those things. But once you've established the boundaries, provide flexibility for your employees to proceed. Complement direction with support, and let people know when they've done a good job, or when you appreciate how they handled a situation.

Encourage Autonomy. Earlier, we said it's important to establish clear boundaries. It is also important to recognize that individuals will adopt different approaches to accomplishing their work. It's important to relinquish control and refrain from micromanaging. Stay focused on the ends rather than the means. And when things don't work as expected, and they often do, don't jump in and provide direction. Rather, provide encouragement for the individual to analyze what happened and determine an alternate approach. Create a culture where people can talk about mistakes, and learn from them rather than become defensive.

Communicate to Build Trust. Effective communication occurs two ways. A successful leader talks with individuals, and groups, about their vision and about their school's successes. But they spend just as much time listening, asking clarifying questions to better understand, and then demonstrating their understanding. They also routinely ask for feedback about their work and regularly ask employees what they need to be successful.

Conversations that build trust and promote autonomy are "real" and "authentic." They are not superficial. When talking with teachers, ask questions specific to the topic at hand. Be specific and thoughtful about feedback. Avoid the use of standardized questions or comments, like, "You're doing a good job," because that doesn't provide any direction and may signal that you're not authentically engaged in the conversation.

Recognize Employees. Show appreciation for work that is well done. Provide specific feedback and acknowledgment of the work. That requires that you know your employees well enough to celebrate in a way that they find rewarding and fulfilling. Always make the celebration about the employee, and understand that not everyone is comfortable with a public acknowledgment of their work.

Assess Yourself

Element	I'm Okay but Need to Work on This Area	I Think I Do a Satisfactory Job	I Go Over and Above in This Area	Evidence for Your Assessment
Involve in planning and decisions.				
Provide professional development and support.				
Balance direction and support.				
Encourage autonomy.				
Communicate to build trust.				
Recognize employees.				

Building a Collaborative School Community

When trust is present, teachers and others are more willing to commit to the vision and to work collaboratively to assure its success. This section will discuss strategies for creating and sustaining a collaborative school, one where people want to work and where families want their children to be educated.

Collaboration is critical to the success of any school. Decisions are better; they have greater support and are more likely to be implemented if they are the result of intentional collaboration with teachers, staff, and parents.

Reflection Point: How do you collaborate with others in your school community?

The days of a solitary leader have disappeared decades ago. But leaders still struggle with how to involve others in decision-making and how to build a viable and successful shared decision-making model. In every school, you can find examples of involvement in decision-making. Sometimes it is systematic, intentional and deals with vital curricular and instructional issues. Other times it's simply a way for the principal to ask about managerial concerns.

There is no formula or perfect method for collaborative decision-making; however, it is most successful when the involvement is authentic, timely, and a routine part of the school's operations.

Benefits and Challenges

There are many benefits of shared decision-making:

- Higher-quality decisions, because more perspectives are considered.
- Increased job satisfaction and morale.
- Heightened sense of empowerment.
- Greater ownership of school goals and priorities when participants have a stake in the decision.
- Improved student achievement because of greater coordination of work among teachers.

On the other hand, there are also challenges or potential obstacles to shared decision-making, which include the following:

- Expanded participation may require more time to make decisions.
- Group dynamics may stifle ideas, leading to "groupthink."
- Polarization around specific points of view.
- People feeling left out or that some have greater access and opportunity to influence decisions.

Assess Yourself

Prompt	Examples from Your School
What benefits of shared decision-making have you seen in your situation?	
What challenges have you experienced?	

Involving others may require more time for planning, time for discussion and analysis of alternatives. But the payoff is better decisions, decisions that have considered alternatives, and decisions that have greater support among stakeholders.

Positive Interpersonal Relationships Are Key

The key to nurturing and sustaining a collaborative culture is to embrace open, honest conversation.

There are often disagreements about direction or priorities in a collaborative environment. That's normal. You need to resist the tendency to point fingers, to blame other people, or to blame factors outside of your school. We don't ever believe that is helpful. The power to monitor implementation and adjust plans lies within the school with teachers and administrators.

We've worked with hundreds of schools in every region of the United States and identified behaviors that can be harmful to your success. Similarly, we've identified behaviors that can support your culture of collaboration.

Inhibitors	*Facilitators*
People are reluctant to share data about things that aren't working.	People are comfortable sharing data about what doesn't work. They are not penalized for doing so.
People use opinions, rather than data, to support their positions.	People support their suggestions with data, facts, and solid logic.
People agree to a decision yet do little to support its success.	People support mutually agreed-upon decisions and work to make the decision succeed.
People seek personal credit for success.	People credit others for success.

(Continued)

(Continued)

Inhibitors	Facilitators
People disagree to improve their own interests rather than to find the best solution or strategy.	People are comfortable disagreeing and are focused on finding the best response to the current issue.
People find blame, seek culprits, rather than identifying causes.	People analyze experiences to identify ways to improve.
People blame others or conditions outside of the school for the lack of success.	People accept full responsibility for successes as well as failures.
The leader avoids critical input and does not ask questions to clarify thinking.	The leader asks lots of questions, challenges thinking, and values discussion and critical insight into issues.

Source: Adapted from Collins (2009).

Assess Yourself

Inhibitors	Percent of Time I See This	Facilitators	Percent of Time I See This
People are reluctant to share data about things that aren't working.		People are comfortable sharing data about what doesn't work. They are not penalized for doing so.	
People use opinions, rather than data, to support their positions.		People support their suggestions with data, facts, and solid logic.	
People agree to a decision yet do little to support its success.		People support mutually agreed-upon decisions and work to make the decision succeed.	
People seek personal credit for success.		People credit others for success.	

Inhibitors	Percent of Time I See This	Facilitators	Percent of Time I See This
People disagree to improve their own interests rather than to find the best solution or strategy.		People are comfortable disagreeing and are focused on finding the best response to the current issue.	
People find blame, seek culprits, rather than identifying causes.		People analyze experiences to identify ways to improve.	
People blame others or conditions outside of the school for the lack of success.		People accept full responsibility for successes as well as failures.	
The leader avoids critical input and does not ask questions to clarify thinking.		The leader asks lots of questions, challenges thinking, and values discussion and critical insight into issues.	

You may recognize some of these behaviors, both positive and negative. That's the thing about groups: they tend to generate strong emotions, especially if it's an issue that people care deeply about. When circumstances change or an issue emerges unexpectedly, the dynamic of the group can change. Your job as a leader is to recognize what is happening and help your team restore balance in their work and decision-making.

Take Action

Facilitators	Strategies for Moving My Stakeholders to This Approach
People are comfortable sharing data about what doesn't work. They are not penalized for doing so.	
People support their suggestions with data, facts, and solid logic.	
People support mutually agreed-upon decisions and work to make the decision succeed.	
People credit others for success.	
People are comfortable disagreeing and are focused on finding the best response to the current issue.	
People analyze experiences to identify ways to improve.	
People accept full responsibility for successes as well as failures.	
The leader asks lots of questions, challenges thinking, and values discussion and critical insight into issues.	

Reflection Point: Do you have formal or informal norms when groups work together? How effective are they?

Establishing Norms for Collaborative Work

The dynamics of groups can be an issue, but one that can be addressed. The most successful collaborative groups develop their own norms for how the group will function and how they will make a decision, which ensures everyone will feel valued. In addition to a decision-making model, they often include things like how to involve everyone in the discussion, how to avoid distractions, and how to record and share decisions that were made. Barbara uses a standard set of norms when working with teachers.

Sample Norms

- We are a team, so we work together rather than competing.
- We respect each other and act appropriately.
- We actively listen to each other, which allows us to authentically contribute our point of view.
- If you disagree, find a positive way to respond without embarrassing the other person.
- Every group member should be able to participate. If one person is talking too much, the other members should give them a signal and move on.
- Making mistakes is normal; it helps us learn.
- The process is just as important as the result. We want to think deeply about our work, elaborate, justify out points, and pose additional questions to promote more thinking.

At times, polarization can occur around specific points of view. Successful groups welcome diverse perspectives but recognize the importance of establishing norms around discussion, use of data or expertise, and entrenched points of view. One middle school improvement team in suburban Phoenix established a norm that when speaking to an issue, you could not cite your own "experience." Individuals needed to cite research or guidance from a professional organization. That limited the use of phrases like, "In my 30 years, I've found . . ."

Finally, people who feel left out or believe that others have greater access and opportunity to influence decisions can create tension. An inclusive group that represents all factions of a school community is critical. We'll provide more information about handling conflict later in this chapter.

Overall, the long-term benefits of collaborative decision-making outweigh the short-term obstacles. When teachers, staff, and families are active partners in decisions about their school, they have more ownership of the school's direction and a greater commitment to its success.

Planning for Collaboration

Developing the structures for collaboration may be as important as the actual collaboration. Too often, groups are formed without thought to membership, the task, or the opportunity to build ownership and empower the staff. We encourage school leaders to be intentional in planning but to make sure they don't do this planning in isolation.

Developing your "plan to collaborate" is one of your first collaborative activities. We suggest using a group that may already exist to help develop the plan.

One of the most important issues is deciding whom to involve. Ask yourself two questions:

1. Who is most closely involved?
2. How much can people contribute? What is their level of expertise? What skills can they provide the group?
3. How diverse are the perspectives and points of view among the membership?

You might also consider other factors in order to facilitate your decision. Hoy and Tarter (2008) suggested that if people have a stake in the outcome and have some level of expertise, they should be involved. If people are indifferent to the outcome and have no expertise, no involvement is needed. Finally, if people are concerned with the outcome but lack expertise or have expertise but are indifferent, then they should have limited participation.

Regardless, who is involved, and how they were selected, will be a very visible indicator of your commitment to authentic collaboration. Avoid selecting friends or known supporters.

Others will see this as "stacking the deck." Strive to include people of diverse points of view. There's a richness of discussion and analysis that comes from differing perspectives. And always be ready to communicate and explain how group members are selected.

Things to Consider

- What is the task?
- Who has a stake in the decision?
- Who should appropriately be involved because of their expertise or their role?
- How will the group be organized?
- What are the group norms?
- How will the decision be made?
- What is the timeline for completion of the task?

Checklist for Formation of Teams

Is the purpose clear? Is the role well-defined?

Is the team needed to address an important issue?

Is membership representative? Is membership appropriate to the task?

Do we have an appropriate format for meeting, both electronic and face-to-face?

Are there agreed-upon norms for operation? For decision-making?

Is there a mechanism to communicate with the larger school community? With other decision-making groups?

What is the process for concluding the team's work?

The bottom line is to be sure the purpose of each team is clear and the roles are well-defined and understood.

Collaborative Team Members

In order to have a collaborative school environment, you must have faculty, staff, and other stakeholders who value working in a collaborative manner. There are six key characteristics of a collaborative team member.

Characteristics of a Collaborative Team Member

- Weighs personal and group goals.
- Focuses on student learning.
- Shows genuine curiosity.
- Respects group members' strengths.
- Balances speaking and listening.
- Handles conflict constructively.

Balances Goals

First, a team member who is collaborative is able to balance their personal and group goals. In other words, they are able to weigh the importance of their own goals and the group's goals and find a way to achieve both and resolve any conflict. For example, if a teacher wants to improve parent and family communication but the overall school goal is to improve student learning, he or she can reframe the goals. From a new perspective, we can address ways to improve student learning, with one particular strategy incorporating family communication and collaboration.

Characteristics of a Collaborative Team Member

- Weighs personal and group goals.
- Focuses on student learning.
- Shows genuine curiosity.
- Respects group members' strengths.
- Balances speaking and listening.
- Handles conflict constructively.

Focuses on Student Learning

An effective collaborator also focuses on student learning. We just discussed the importance of stakeholders balancing personal and group goals. Unfortunately, it is very easy to become distracted by personal agendas. All too frequently, we've heard issues portrayed as affecting students when in fact it was an issue affecting an individual teacher or group of teachers.

At a recent workshop about developing a remediation plan for at-risk students, two teachers began to argue about technology and their own scheduling needs. The two continued to bicker for some time, until the principal reminded everyone that the purpose of the remediation classes was to positively affect student learning for their neediest students. By reframing the conversation to a focus on student learning, the group was able to move forward.

Ask the Question

Barbara worked with a principal whose teachers struggled to focus on student learning. He put up a poster on his door: "How does what you want/want to do **positively** impact student learning?" If they couldn't answer it effectively, the answer was no!

Shows Curiosity

Next, a skilled collaborator shows genuine curiosity. Rather than being a passive participant during collaborative work, these colleagues are eager to learn. They ask questions, probe for more information, and share their own ideas when appropriate.

> **Sample Questions That Reflect Curiosity**
>
> ♦ Have you seen that idea used in a classroom? What did you think?
> ♦ Have you used it in your own classroom? How did it work?
> ♦ Where did you hear about the idea? How can I learn more?
> ♦ What adaptations do you think would help us improve student learning? Why?

Respects Strengths

Closely tied to the skill of curiosity is that a good collaborator respects the strengths of others in the group. Unfortunately, there are times in education that an atmosphere of competition, particularly regarding standardized test scores or ratings, overshadows any collaborative work. In that case, leaders must work to shift the overall atmosphere from competition to cooperation. One facet of that process is the ability of team members to respect each other. Opportunities to identify and reinforce strengths of other group members should be a regular part of the collaborative process. A true collaborator not only recognizes the strengths of others but also validates those strengths and encourages others to do the same.

Personality Characteristic	Value for Collaboration
Cautious	Ensures we look at all possibilities rather than rushing into a decision
Action-oriented	Ensures a final decision will be made
Creative	Ensures we "think out of the box" and look at a variety of options

Personality Characteristic	Value for Collaboration
Friendly	Helps smooth over conflicts and facilitate teamwork
Straightforward	Cuts through the clutter and "noise" to get to the main points(s)

Speaks and Listens

Next, a stakeholder who collaborates well with others balances how much they speak and how much they listen. We've all been in groups where one person dominates a conversation. You might think this does not happen as often in a virtual setting, but it can. We've seen teachers take over a Zoom meeting, dominate a chat, or overwhelm a shared-document platform with information. Barbara once saw a sign: *Nature gave us two ears and one mouth so we could listen twice as much as we speak.* That's not a bad guide. Skilled collaborators share information but listen to be sure they are contributing in a positive way.

How to Listen Effectively

- Look at the speaker even when they are not looking at you.
- Be attentive to the conversation rather than multitasking.
- Ask questions to clarify what you heard.
- Take notes or create a mind map to record ideas and make connections.
- Help everyone stay on task. Redirect chats that are off-task or off-topic and suggest holding the information for a later time.

Handles Conflict

Although there can be conflict in any collaborative work, it can be intensified in times of stress or conflict. If you use virtual options for meeting, team members may not be able to see nonverbal cues; they can take the comments as ones that are more personal than normal. For example, if a teacher comments in a chat, "I think we all just need to pay attention to our struggling students," in a face-to-face setting, other teachers may realize he is expressing frustration.

It's also easy for conflict to escalate when people quickly respond without reflecting on others' comments. That's why norms about listening, asking questions, and being open to all points of view are important.

There are several ways to minimize conflict and handle it appropriately, most of which should be modeled and organized by the leader. First, we want to emphasize the importance of group norms for both the process and decision-making. One team in a suburban Chicago middle school began every meeting by reviewing their norms and selecting one for focus during each meeting. They found that the gentle reminder helped keep the norms present.

You can also provide a non-distracting method for sharing complaints. Many groups adopt a system to record "off-topic" issues or questions for later discussion, post those on a nearby bulletin board, and return to them later.

It's also helpful to end every meeting by reviewing what was discussed, any decisions that were made, and any assignments members may have prior to the next meeting. One group Ron worked with always identified what would be shared and how the sharing would occur. This helped protect the integrity of the group and minimize side conversations that would harm interpersonal relations among members.

Other Ways to Minimize Conflict

Don't ignore conflict.
Provide an option for written feedback.

> Don't show favoritism.
> Get to know your group individually.
> Don't blame.

Assessing Strengths and Challenges

As you are working with your teachers and other stakeholders to develop their collaboration skills, consider each desired characteristic and note the strengths and challenges of each group member, which will allow you and other leaders to facilitate positive collaboration.

Teacher Self-Assess: Group Collaboration

Element	I'm Okay but Need to Work on This Area	I Think I Do a Satisfactory Job	I Go Over and Above in This Area	Evidence for Your Assessment
Weighs personal and group goals				
Focuses on student learning				
Shows genuine curiosity				
Respects strengths of group members				
Balances speaking and listening				
Handles conflict constructively				
Additional input				

As you work to build ownership, you will want to assess how you're doing on developing and sustaining collaborative efforts. Assessments allow you to make short-term and long-term adjustments, as well as measuring the success of your group(s). We recommend using a two-part process. First, based on standard criteria, each group member assesses whether the team reached the goal, is making progress, or needs work. They should write an example or justification of their choices. Next, provide an open-ended portion so they can provide any other input.

Final Thoughts

No leader wants to micromanage their school. Doing so will overwhelm you and, because you can't possibly anticipate every need, make you less successful. That's why creating a school where employees feel empowered through their ownership of the school's vision and mission is so important. Building an empowered school takes time, but there are specific things a leader can do to support and nurture such empowerment.

8

Building Morale through Modeling

> Motivation Connection:
> When you model for those around you, you impact their motivation, whether positive or negative. Choose positive.

One of Ron's friends once said, "What a principal pays attention to becomes important." That's an important lesson for any leader. Every leader's behavior is a model for those around them. If they're calm, others are more likely to be calm. If they plan thoughtfully, others will see that as a value. In other words, what you model can affect the motivation of others.

That's why the way a leader goes about their work, and the values they model, are so critical. In this section we'll discuss the importance of focusing on yourself as a leader, how to manage the use of time, how to assure work–life balance, and how to model professional learning.

Few jobs are as complex and involve as many different responsibilities as the school principalship. Managing them can, at times, seem overwhelming, and principals often find themselves caught up in necessary but less-important tasks.

It's hard for the public, or even the staff, to understand that a principal's work continues even when crises or special events occur. Managing the tasks is important because principals want to be seen as "staying on top" of things. Their reputation, and that of their school, is often directly linked to their ability to juggle multiple priorities and accomplish multiple tasks at the same time.

The same is true for teachers. They have complex jobs with multiple responsibilities. For everyone, there is an ongoing challenge to manage time and to assure a healthy work–life balance, which affects motivation. Leaders need to model the importance of both time management and work–life balance and expect their teachers to do the same.

Reflection Point: On a 1–10 scale, how balanced do you feel your work and life are now? Why?

Model Time Management

A recent study found that when the boundaries between work and personal lives have become less clear (McGregor, 2020), employees often work longer hours and are expected to assume additional responsibilities, including planning for potential remote learning or handling health crises. That's created an almost-universal recognition that managing time, and managing the boundaries between work and personal lives, is an essential skill for every school leader. The way a leader handles this need creates a model for those that work with them.

Despite the almost-universal recognition that leaders need to manage their time wisely, there is little research on practices that are most effective. What is known is that how you manage time affects job performance, your stress level, and your personal life (Claessens, van Eerde, Rutte, & Roe, 2007).

Time management consists of three behaviors: setting goals and priorities, the mechanics of organizing and doing one's job, and each individual's unique style and preferences (Macan, 1994). In other words, what works for one leader may not be useful for another. This recognition of the idiosyncratic nature of time management means there are all sorts of strategies to effective time management. The most effective approach is the one that works best for an individual leader.

While the research on time management is meager, all sorts of time management tools and strategies emerge from the literature.

These strategies generally include developing a clear set of priorities, organizing your tasks, and identifying specific techniques to complete those tasks.

Step 1: Assess Where You Are and How You Spend Time

It's likely that you need to rebalance the use of time as a result of the new responsibilities associated with remote learning.

Virtually, all recommendations about time management suggest beginning with an assessment of your work and priorities. The first step is to recognize the strengths and challenges of your current time management. Clarifying where you are is an important step in beginning to change your situation. Take a few minutes and assess your current situation.

The list of challenges, while often long, is most often not nearly as out of control as you think. Taking time to assess the current situation is often helpful in gaining "a dose of reality" and control about your situation.

Next, identify your most important, or essential, responsibilities. Then describe the tasks associated with those responsibilities. Covey (1996) describes these as the "big rocks" and suggests in *First Things First* that these tasks must always be taken care of first before the other smaller and less-important tasks. These top priorities must be scheduled, or they will be neglected. For principals, they are the "big rocks" that most often drive student learning. While every school is a little different, those priorities generally revolve around improving instruction and student learning.

What are the essential tasks that must be attended to in order to assure a quality educational program for your students? Now, create a vision of how you want to spend your time. Imagine a day in which you are relaxed and productive. For example, if your work was completely effective, efficient, and balanced, how would you spend your time?

Here are some strategies that can help with this task:

- ♦ Select a week and use a journal to record how you spend time. This will help you identify how much you can get done and identify the most useful time, as well as the most unproductive, or distracting, time.

- Take the first 30 minutes of every day to plan your day. Don't start until the plan is completed. This activity helps focus the day and what you want to accomplish.
- Before every scheduled call or meeting, take a couple of minutes and clarify what you want to accomplish. It helps to identify what success looks like during the call or meeting. Similarly, take five minutes following every call or meeting to reflect and determine if you achieved the results you desired, and to clarify next steps.
- Think about patterns in your day. For example, the beginning of the day can be an important time to connect with teachers and students. How will you continue those connections while working remotely? What other patterns during the day need to be addressed? Anticipate those patterns and allot time for these visits.
- If unannounced calls or texts arrive, think about how you will manage them. Develop a system for monitoring and responding to unexpected requests.

Take Action: Choose one of the strategies, and assess your current situation.

Step 2: Make a Mental Adjustment

Many principals feel overwhelmed with everything they need to do. Our thoughts drive our feelings and actions. We've found it helpful if we want to make a change to start with an adjustment in how we think about what we are doing.

From Negative Thought	To Positive Thought
I'll never be able to keep up with every teacher's message.	I'll reply to every teacher's message in a timely manner every day.
It's impossible to keep everyone happy.	Every interaction I have with people will be sincere, regardless of their behavior.

Focus on the positive progress you make each day, whether it is effectively delegating a task or responding to a teacher's need for additional support with technology. Give credit to others, and to yourself, for the things you accomplish each day. One principal told Ron he always ended the day making a list of the things that were accomplished and creating a list of things to focus on the next day.

- **Control Self-Interruption.** There are lots of ways to distract yourself from what needs to be done. Distraction is most likely to occur when the task is unpleasant or requires energy or skills you lack at that moment. Distraction may even come from the organization of the office or your workspace. Materials needed for a task should be organized and easily accessible. If the interruption is mental fatigue, move around and stretch, take a short walk, eat a healthy snack, or meditate for a few minutes. Some principals actually schedule time for high-priority work.
- **Do, Delegate, or Delete.** A critical mental adjustment is to recognize that every task doesn't require the principal to complete it. Think about the daily routine and consider what may detract from your productivity. Identify the tasks that you really must do, those that can be delegated to someone else and those that don't need to be done. This critical assessment often identifies nonessential tasks that detract from accomplishing the most essential tasks.
- **Only Handle It Once (OHIO).** One of the most prevalent time management suggestions is to read an email, memo, or message only once. Reading them multiple times multiplies the time you spend. It's more efficient to take a minute and decide what to do and move it out of your inbox or off your desk. The only exception should be tasks that are delegated to another person.
- **Just Say No.** One of the hardest things for many leaders to do is to say no. Leaders worry that people's feelings will be hurt or they will be seen as less competent. Four questions help you master the art of saying no:
    - ♦ Am I capable and qualified to do what's being asked?
    - ♦ Do I have time for this task or activity?
    - ♦ Do I want to do this activity?
    - ♦ What are the ramifications of saying no?

Not Everything Is an Emergency. Remember that most emergencies are only in the eye of the beholder. Not every problem is a crisis, particularly if the problem resulted from someone else's poor planning. Of course, authentic emergencies occur and you must respond, but in many cases, so-called emergencies do not require immediate attention. Work toward minimizing urgent tasks.

Take Care of Yourself. It's an old adage, but caregivers need to take care of themselves so that they can care for others. School leaders are important caregivers, especially when there's an abrupt change to school operations, like moving to remote learning.

> Take Action: Choose one of the suggestions just mentioned and try it. How did it work? How can you adjust it for your needs?

Too often, the demands of the job mean that little time is available to devote to your own professional learning. As we've learned the past few years, it's hard to predict the future. But what we know is that schools, and their leaders, will continue to be buffeted by a whole set of issues.

Every school leader knows that change is part of the job. But change can be difficult, particularly when it occurs suddenly and with little advance notice. It often requires changing old habits and adjusting perspectives, and an even more complex workload. But there are other needs as well, like the balance between work and your personal life or dealing with the challenge of curricular or instructional change.

Because the principalship is a demanding job, it is important that principals invest in their own health, their personal relationships, and their interests and avocations. Almost all principals are exhausted at the end of the day, and good time management includes finding time for yourself and managing your own physical, emotional, mental, and spiritual resources. The very best, most effective caregivers are those that pay attention to their own needs and take care of their own physical and emotional health. Here are some commonsense suggestions (Marshall, 2008).

- Exercise faithfully (three times a week recommended).
- Eat the right foods, starting with a healthy breakfast.
- Get enough sleep.
- Carve out time for relaxation and fun.
- Build a support system of friends, mentors, and significant others.
- Orchestrate small and large wins to provide an extra shot of optimism and energy. Be comfortable rewarding yourself.

Step 3: Create or Identify Structures to Support Your Plan

The third step in good time management is to create a set of regular, consistent structures that will support a productive day. There is no one perfect strategy—except the one that works for you. However, there are several strategies that other principals have found effective.

Here are other ideas worthy of consideration.

Use a Journal. Several principals we know maintain a running journal, either electronic or on paper, to take notes from meetings, calls, and emails and create a "to-do" list. This ensures that everything is in one place rather than on multiple pieces of paper or multiple sticky notes. A journal also makes it easy to look back and find ideas and tasks that emerged at earlier meetings.

Maintain a Single Calendar. Nothing can be more confusing and lead to missed commitments than the use of multiple calendars. An Oregon principal puts tasks she wants to accomplish on her calendar as a reminder. Synching electronic calendars to computers that maintain your calendar should be a daily function.

Take Control of Email/Texts. Managing email or texts can be a major time management issue. Check them at set times, not all the time. Morgenstern (2005) encourages managers to not check it before 10:00 a.m. She suggests that checking email first thing each day allows the email to set the day's agenda. Rather than responding to email, she encouraged using the first two hours of each day to work on your most important priorities rather than acting on the most recent request. Turn off the automatic notification of your email or texting program. When it beeps, it distracts you from your work.

Establish Norms around Access. When working in a remote environment, it can feel like everyone has access all the time. The number of emails and texts can be overwhelming. While everyone wants to be responsive, a literal open door can lead to fragmentation of your day. Identify a quiet time each day to respond to email. Don't reinforce the idea that you respond the moment you receive a message. Also be clear about interruptions. Access is important, but uninterrupted time to accomplish tasks is also important. Consider setting blocks of time when you will not be interrupted except in emergencies.

Schedule a "To-Do" Meeting. Schedule a short, regular meeting with your leadership team to review key activities and delegate items to others in the team. You may do this through regular written communication instead of a meeting.

Take Action: Choose one of the suggestions and try it. How did it work? How can you adjust it for your needs?

Successful leaders develop systems for managing their time. Once you develop your own system, talk about it with others. Model its use and describe how it helps you manage your day. Don't impose your system on others, but by modeling the use of a plan, you signal the importance of managing time for every person you work with.

Model Work–Life Balance

Finding the balance between personal and professional responsibilities is a struggle for many school leaders. The job is complex. The day is long and filled with expectations from both senior leadership in the district and from families and the community (Whitaker, 1996). The idea that school leaders are available any time, any day of the week adds stress, especially with the ready access to technology.

Work–life balance is also important for your teachers. By modeling balance in your own life, you signal them that they should also develop a plan for balance. Encourage every employee to figure out what works for them, and support them in that plan. Make sure families and the community understand that you are supportive of your teachers and other employees maintaining work–life balance.

While the importance of work–life balance is well-documented, just like time management, there is no single strategy or approach that works for everyone. Balance, in the truest sense of the word, is not about compartmentalizing your life. As David Allen in *Getting Things Done* (2015) notes, it's about being appropriately engaged with what you are doing in the moment.

Work–life balance doesn't necessarily mean there is an equal division between the two. Individual interests, goals, obligations, and commitments mean that the balance is more fluid and shifts over time. But the evidence is clear that work–life balance positively affects individuals as well as the organizations where they work.

Work–life balance improves overall morale in your school. Improved morale makes your school an attractive place to work and will help in recruiting teachers.

Here's a summary of the benefits.

Benefits for the Individual	*Benefits for the School*
♦ Work–life balance contributes to a healthier life. ♦ Stress is reduced when there is balance. ♦ Relationships improve both on the job and away from the job. ♦ Your work, as well as your personal life, is more satisfying.	♦ There is increased productivity and commitment at work. ♦ Teamwork and communication are improved. ♦ Overall organizational stress is reduced. ♦ The collective morale improves.

So how do you go about assuring greater balance between work and your personal life? Four strategies have been found helpful. They are all about being intentional about how you prioritize your day and activities.

Understand Yourself

In order to achieve work–life balance, you need to think about yourself, your patterns, and your aspirations. Values and beliefs shape our actions and impact our personal set of life experiences. Here are some suggestions for understanding yourself.

- *Define what "greater balance" means for you.* What would it look like if it was achieved? Who else should be part of the conversation about work–life balance?
- *Think about what you value.* Being clear about your values is one key to establishing balance, or at least understanding why you don't have balance. A conflict in values can create stress and disrupt the balance we seek. For example, you may value getting to work early, but also value spending a little time with your spouse, children, or significant other before your day begins. Perhaps you value finishing your work before you leave for the day, but also value attending your children's after-school activities or being available to help with childcare or household chores.
- *Identify your patterns.* Think about how you organize your day. What things always get accomplished and what things deferred? What choices do you make about sleep, diet, and exercise? Do you schedule breakfast meetings, or do you reserve that time for transitioning from personal time to work?
- *Understand your natural workday rhythms.* People have their own natural rhythms. Identify your rhythms and patterns during the day. Some people prefer an unstructured start to the day; others prefer to jump right into their work. Figure out your rhythms, and structure your work around those natural patterns. Pay attention to your patterns over the day.

Set Realistic Goals and Expectations

Take Action: Sketch out your ideal day. Be sure it reflects your values and the natural rhythm of your day.

Finding work–life balance is about setting priorities and managing time (Graham, 2002; Uscher, 2011). Our perceptions, attitudes, and assumptions often shape the expectations we have for ourselves. Here are some suggestions for setting realistic goals.

- *Check out assumptions about your work.* Talk with your supervisor about priorities and balance. Help your supervisor understand the right balance for your life and how that balance can be achieved. We often set our unrealistic standards for our own performance. Good supervisors know the importance of work–life balance and how a lack of balance can negatively impact an individual's work and the health of the entire organization.
- *Talk with your family or significant other* about priorities and schedules. Much of the stress about work–life balance is a result of tension with those we care about the most. Talking about the issues and being open to finding solutions helps lessen the stress.
- *Include time for yourself* and your own personal interests among your goals. Be sure to allow time for adequate sleep and exercise.

Managing Work–Life Balance

Take Action: Revisit your ideal day. Now, let's be practical. Given what you have to do, blend the ideal and the real to create a manageable plan.

Even with realistic goals and an understanding of your own values, managing work–life balance can be a challenge. Here's advice from others about work–life balance.

- *Build time for yourself into your schedule.* When you plan your week, include time for exercise, for hobbies or activities, for family and friends. Actually, add it to the schedule just like any other professional commitment. Most importantly, "be proactive about scheduling." When leaders don't take care of themselves and recognize

the need for balance, it negatively impacts the whole organization.
- ♦ *Make boundaries clear.* Negotiate, and legitimize, boundaries between work and your personal life. Be really clear about when you are available for work activities and the time your preserve for family and personal time. Take control of your day and week. There may be times during the day when your door is closed and you're working on projects, other times when you are available. The same is true for your personal and family time. Give yourself permission to delay responding to texts or email.
- ♦ *Identify a mentor, coach, or friend with whom you can talk.* Being a leader, particularly in a small school, can be an isolated job. There's evidence that leaders need someone with whom they can talk and share problems, including frustrations about work–life balance. The person must be someone you trust, and there is some evidence that a person outside of education, who doesn't share the same expectations, can be the best listener.
- ♦ *Pay attention to sleep, exercise, and diet.* Busy people often neglect sleep and exercise and may not eat regularly, or make unhealthy choices about what they eat. Be attentive to the need for adequate sleep, and build time for exercise, even a walk around the outside of the school, into your schedule. Don't grab lunch "on the run" or eat while working on other things. Instead, take short mental breaks, eat a healthy snack, and drink plenty of water.
- ♦ *Talk with your partner.* The quality of your personal relationships impacts everyone around you. Talk openly with your partner about work–life balance, about priorities, about scheduling, and about how to support one another.
- ♦ *Stop doing some things.* Analyze your schedule and your activities. Identify things that you don't need to do or don't need to do as frequently. Give yourself permission to drop them from your routine.
- ♦ *Delegate and/or divide work.* Often, a leader thinks they must do everything or respond to every request. They often

worry about losing control. There are often others in your school who can do some of the work. Some people enjoy the opportunity to learn a new task, or perhaps they aspire to be a school leader and want some experience with leadership tasks. Become comfortable delegating tasks or subdividing the work among several people.

Take Action: Revisit your sketch of day. Build in any of the preceding strategies to make it even more manageable for you.

Communicate, Communicate, Communicate

While planning is helpful to work–life balance, even more helpful is communication with your supervisor, those you work with, and with your spouse or significant other. In the absence of communication, others are left to form their own opinions and make their own judgments. Here are some other communication tips from the University of Maine (Graham, 2002).

Final Tips

Remember that work–life balance is not a static event. You don't develop a plan one time. It's a process that evolves and changes. Be willing to revise your plans and change as needed. But be intentional about talking with family and others, and about keeping time each week, or month, for things like exercise, family activities, or personal interests.

Model Continuous Learning

Every year we work with dozens of principals, and we've come to appreciate the challenges they face. Principals are asked to solve some of the most complex and contentious issues in schooling, and over the past few years, many have been tasked with moving their school to a totally remote or hybrid learning model and deal with multiple health-care challenges. We marvel at their energy and their capacity for change. From these principals, we've learned things you can do to continue your own learning. *Keep in mind, when you continue your own learning and model it for your teachers, you help them feel valued and successful, which positively impacts their motivation.*

Be a continuous learner.

- Be intellectually curious. Read a lot and think a lot about current and emerging trends. Be open to ways to improve your school even when things are going well. There is a lot of information online about how schools responded to remote learning. Spend time with traditional publications and online, in education and in other fields, to learn about trends and new ideas and to promote your own thinking.
- Cultivate a critical friend, someone outside your school or outside education. Such a friend can provide a fresh perspective on issues you face.
- Actively participate in every professional development activity with your teachers. Value the opportunity to learn from them, to reflect on your learning, and to apply it in your work. Be present. Be engaged. Show your teachers that you value continuous learning.
- Talk with others about what you read, what you've watched, and what you've learned. When you share your learning model, it emphasizes the importance of learning. Often, the most valuable sharing comes from comments you make when talking with individuals or small groups of teachers rather than a presentation at a staff meeting.
- Organize a discussion group with other principals. Identify a shared interest or select a book of interest and commit to sharing your thinking and ideas. Zoom or other online platforms can provide a structure for online book study.
- Join the online communities of your professional association (NAESP, NASSP, ASCD), and tap into the advice they provide.
- Enjoy what you do. Relish the impact that principals have on the education of students in their school. When the enjoyment fades, find ways to reinvigorate your passion, and model the importance of continuous learning.

> Take Action: Which of the strategies are most helpful to you? Which do you want to implement? Which do you want to share with your teachers?

The good news is that technology has made staying connected far easier than it has ever been. Use some of the online options, or simply use your computer's search engine to find an abundance of information about the experience of other schools in the move to remote learning.

Final Thoughts

What school leaders do, how they act, and what they talk about send more powerful signals to their teachers and community about values and beliefs than anything they say. Your actions impact the motivation of your faculty and staff. School leaders are models for those who work in their schools, and it's important to model behaviors that support a healthy balance between work and personal life and the desire for continuous learning. Schools are places of learning, and school leaders must model the importance of learning.

9

Challenges and Concerns

> Motivation Connection: When addressing intrinsic motivation, you'll want to expand leadership capacity, address negative resistance, and focus on dealing with ongoing change.

Despite the best of plans, you'll face challenges and obstacles in any effort to improve motivation and morale. The first chapters provided an overview of strategies for improvement, including creating a growth mindset and resilience, building a trusting climate, and cultivating ownership along with empowerment. This chapter discusses three issues that are often present, issues that can inhibit your efforts.

First, we'll examine how to expand leadership capacity. That's important because a broad base of leadership is often accompanied by a shared commitment to change and improvement. Next, we'll look at resistance and how to deal with the most destructive form of resistance. Resistance is almost always present, but most of it can be addressed with adequate information and time to accept the change. Finally, the chapter will discuss how a leader deals with the perpetual change in the political, social, and economic environment, changes that can dramatically impact a school.

> Reflection Point: Which of these three areas is your biggest challenge?

How Do I Build Leadership Capacity in My School?

Solitary leadership doesn't work very well. It can achieve short-term compliance but doesn't build long-term commitment. When the leader changes, the compliance stops.

A far more effective strategy is for a school leader to systematically build leadership capacity among the staff. Not everyone wants to be a "formal" leader, but everyone can lead. Cultivating capacity among the staff expands participation, empowers and increases collective knowledge, and increases motivation and improves morale (Newton, 2017; Nelson & Dunsmore, 2018).

Most teachers are motivated by a deep desire to become better teachers and to work with their colleagues to improve their schools. It's important to tap into that motivation to support your efforts at improving your school.

What a Leader Can Do

Expanding leadership capacity doesn't occur simply by tapping a teacher to head a new committee. Rather, it comes from identifying talented people, their interests and strengths, and providing opportunities for them to use those talents.

Leadership emerges in multiple ways and not from being designated a formal leader. It may emerge from participation in targeted professional development, from work on a collaborative team, or from investigating a problem and researching possible solutions.

School leaders can grow and nurture leadership capacity by doing these five things.

1. **Know Your Teachers and Their Work.** It's important to get out of the office and get to know what's going on in classrooms and at grade-level or team meetings. Becoming engaged in the authentic work of teachers, being present when they're teaching, collaborating, and problem-solving will provide a leader with insight into the frustrations of teachers, the joys of their work, and the challenges they face. Being able to speak from "authentic" experience rather than from your office experience allows you to match talent

with interests. Skilled teachers want to work on "real" instructional problems, and a principal with "real" experience, able to use the "real" language, will be valued.

2. **Move Beyond Formal Leaders**. In many schools, there are formal and informal leaders designated as assistant principals, department heads, or grade-level chair. When expanding capacity, it's important to move beyond those formal leaders. Most teachers don't want to be involved in managerial tasks, like ordering supplies or building schedules. What they value is the chance to work on authentic instructional issues. That's motivating. Don't assume that the person who is skilled at managerial tasks will be the best fit for every leadership role.

3. **Create Welcoming Spaces**. Establish healthy boundaries for communication. Model confidentiality, and respect a teacher's privacy when they share a problem or concern. Teachers want to solve problems, but first, the problem has to be identified. Too often, teachers are reluctant to share concerns because they worry they will be blamed. You want people to step forward and identify problems. That's the only way they can be addressed.

4. **Ask Difficult Questions**. A leader shouldn't wait for problems to be identified by others. A leader's job is not just to solve problems but also to identify problems by asking difficult questions. Challenge long-standing norms. Ask why instructional challenges are handled the way they are. This can stimulate new thinking and provide an opportunity for teachers to step forward and investigate and address the issue.

5. **Provide Professional Development**. Too often, professional development (PD) is something done to fulfill a district mandate or contractual requirement. When building leadership capacity, it's important to tailor the PD to the interests and needs of individual teachers. We understand the need for school-wide training on issues, but supplement that with an opportunity for specific, targeted PD. It might involve online activities or attendance at a conference, or even participation on

a district-wide committee. Recognize the power of PD aligned with teacher interests to motivate teachers and improve morale.

Assess Yourself

Element	I'm Okay but Need to Work on This Area	I Think I Do a Satisfactory Job	I Go Over and Above in This Area	Evidence for Your Assessment
Know your teachers and their work.				
Move beyond formal leaders.				
Create welcoming spaces.				
Ask difficult questions.				
Provide professional development.				

How Should I Deal with Resistance?

One of the biggest challenges you will face is the resistance that emerges from teachers. It may manifest itself through the voice of a single highly vocal, resistant teacher, or more subtly through the chatter from a small group of teachers or other staff.

Addressing the Resistance

Not everyone who resists does so because of ulterior motives. Often, there is a conflict between their personal beliefs and values and the proposed changes. In Michigan, many educators and parents opposed the idea of increasing the mathematics requirement for high school graduation. A survey found that many of those resisting the idea were concerned that the new requirement would lead to more students dropping out of school. Their motives were anchored in concern for students, not outright resistance to the idea. As the new requirements were implemented, much of the resistance faded when students were provided additional academic support, multiple opportunities to succeed, and different instructional approaches.

While some people resist just to resist, most don't. They are genuinely concerned about the proposed change. They either don't see the value in the change or they have concerns about how successful the change will be.

Leaders need to recognize the diverse feelings and concerns when you begin to work on any improvement plan. Individuals progress through the stages in a developmental manner. Not everyone will move at the same pace or have the same intensity of feeling.

As you work to improve motivation and morale, personal concerns about the details of plans are often the first to emerge. Once you're underway, teachers become more interested in the effects of the change on students and on their classrooms.

What to Do with a Toxic Teacher

But occasionally, there is one individual who resists in a way that disrupts the entire school and detracts from the work of other teachers and staff. They're often toxic, because in addition to causing disgruntlement in the workplace, they also spread their disgruntlement to others.

What a Leader Can Do

Here are six steps experts recommend for managing the toxic employee (Gallo, 2016).

- **Dig Deeper.** Always take a close look at the behavior and what might be causing it. It may be because of factors outside of school or unhappiness with colleagues or opportunities for advancement. This information may be used to coach the teacher or suggest resources such as the employee assistance program.

- **Provide Direct Feedback.** Toxic employees may be oblivious to their behavior and its effect on the school and other employees. Porath (2016) suggests that they may be too focused on their own needs and it may be necessary to let them know how annoying they are. Be explicit and cite examples. Just don't dwell on it and allow them to control the conversation. In addition, Porath found that 4 percent of people engage in this kind of behavior because they think they can get away with it and they think it is just fun.
- **Explain Consequences.** Let the teacher know about the costs of their continued behavior. It may mean limited opportunity for professional development or travel to conferences or even transfer or dismissal. In some states, non-tenured teachers can be dismissed without providing a reason.
- **Understand That Some People Don't Change.** It's always good to be optimistic and to support and encourage employees. But that doesn't work with everyone. If that's the case, you may need to talk with your human resources office about next steps.
- **Document Everything.** As with all personnel issues, be sure and document all your conversations, your meetings and suggestions for improvement. This helps establish a pattern of behavior.
- **Isolate the Toxic Person and "Immunize" the Team.** If the toxic behavior persists and the person remains in your school, you can isolate them and minimize their impact. Don't assign them a role in your planning. Don't include them in any groups planning implementation or professional development. If you organize work groups, minimize their role, if any. You can rearrange rooms, schedule fewer meetings, and lessen the contact with colleagues. If other employees come to you about their toxic colleague, hold one-on-one conversations, but be discreet and coach them on how to minimize contact and interaction.
- **Don't Get Distracted.** Finally, a toxic teacher has a way of consuming your time and energy. Don't allow that to

happen. Find time to counteract their behavior by working and interacting with employees who are supportive and engaged. And of course, take care of your own work–life balance, something discussed later in this chapter.

A truly toxic teacher is rare. But when one is present, it can undermine your efforts to improve motivation and morale. There's some evidence that when the leader fails to deal with the

Assess Yourself

Element	I'm Okay but Need to Work on This Area	I Think I Do a Satisfactory Job	I Go Over and Above in This Area	Evidence for Your Assessment
Dig deeper.				
Provide deeper feedback.				
Explain consequences.				
Understand that some people don't change.				
Document everything.				
Isolate the toxic person and "immunize" the team.				
Don't get distracted.				

issue, it has a negative effect on both motivation and morale. Other employees want to know why the leader doesn't act and why the person is allowed to undermine the efforts of the rest of the staff.

Maintain Focus on Students

It seems so obvious to always think about students first. But we've found that when complex and difficult issues arise, student interests are often secondary to the interests of teachers, parents, or community. Part of the problem is that everything that people want to do is always described as being "in the best interests of students." Often, diametrically opposed ideas are both described that way.

William Roberts, Principal of Los Altos High School in Hacienda Heights, California, led significant changes in his school's program. He said that he always asked his staff, "How would you want your child to be treated? What would you want their program to be like?" He found that for many of his teachers, those questions forced them to consider the needs of their students through the perspective of a parent. That question changed the conversation.

Model Continuous Learning

We work with dozens of school leaders, and we've come to appreciate the challenges they face. Principals are asked to solve some of the most complex and contentious issues in schooling, and over the past few years, many have been tasked with moving their school to a totally remote or hybrid learning model and deal with multiple health-care challenges.

We marvel at their energy and their capacity for change. From these leaders, we've learned how very important it is to continue your own learning. One thing is certain: the environment in which schools operate will continue to change, and principals will be expected to respond and adapt. Keep in mind, when you continue your own learning and model it for your teachers, you help them feel valued and successful, which positively impacts their motivation.

Be a continuous learner.

- Be intellectually curious. Read a lot and think a lot about current and emerging trends. Be open to ways to improve your school even when things are going well. There is a lot of information online about how schools responded to remote learning. Spend time with traditional publications and online, in education and in other fields, to learn about trends and new ideas and to promote your own thinking.
- Cultivate a critical friend or two, someone outside your school or outside education. Such a friend can provide a fresh perspective on issues you face.
- Actively participate in every professional development activity with your teachers. Value the opportunity to learn from them, to reflect on your learning, and to apply it in your work. Be present. Be engaged. Show your teachers that you value continuous learning.
- Talk with others about what you read, what you've watched, and what you've learned. When you share your learning model, it emphasizes the importance of learning. Often, the most valuable sharing comes from comments you make when talking with individuals or small groups of teachers rather than a presentation at a staff meeting.
- Organize a discussion group with other principals. Identify a shared interest or select a book of interest, and commit to sharing your thinking and ideas. Zoom or other online platforms can provide a structure for online book study.
- Join the online communities of your professional association (NAESP, NASSP, ASCD), and tap into the advice they provide.
- Enjoy what you do. Relish the impact that principals have on the education of students in their school. When the enjoyment fades, find ways to reinvigorate your passion and model the importance of continuous learning.

The good news is that technology has made staying connected far easier than it has ever been. Use some of the online options or

> Take Action: Which of the strategies are most helpful to you? Which do you want to implement? Which do you want to share with your teachers?

simply use your computer's search engine to find an abundance of information about the experience of other schools in the move to remote learning.

A Final Thought

This chapter discussed three common issues that impact a leader's ability to improve motivation and morale. Because a leader can't do everything and isn't an expert in everything, it's important to expand leadership capacity among the entire staff. Teachers are committed to doing their best and improving their schools. It's important to tap into that commitment. At the same time, there is often resistance to change, and it's important to recognize the kind of resistance, especially when it negatively impacts your school. Finally, as we discussed earlier about balancing work and personal lives, leaders must care for themselves. One way to do that is to attend to their own learning, to read widely, and to stay attuned to the issues and trends that may impact their school.

References

Allen, D. (2001). *Getting things done: The art of stress-free productivity*. New York: Viking.

Anderson, A. (2013). Work-life balance: 5 ways to turn it from the ultimate oxymoron into a real plan. *Forbes Magazine*. Retrieved from www.forbes.com/sites/amyanderson/2013/07/26/work-life-balance-the-ultimate-oxymoron-or-5-tips-to-help-you-achieve-better-worklife-balance/?sh=3f017ff85841

Behrstock, E., & Clifford, M. (2009). *Leading Gen Y teachers: Emerging strategies for school leaders*. Washington, DC: National Comprehensive Center for Teacher Quality.

Blackburn, B. R. (2005). *Classroom motivation from A to Z: How to engage your students in learning*. Larchmont, NY: Eye on Education.

Blackburn, B. R. (2016). *Motivating struggling learners: Ten strategies for student success*. New York: Routledge.

Bolman, L., & Deal, T. (2021). *Reframing organizations: Artistry, choice and leadership* (7th ed.). Hoboken, NY: John Wiley & Sons, Inc.

Booher, M. (2021). *Conscious culture: A game plan to build a great workplace*. Loveland, OH: Influencer Network Media.

Bosworth, P. (2022). *How to empower employees in the workplace—8 tips*. Retrieved online from https://leadershipchoice.com/empower-employees-in-the-workplace/

Brown, B. (2018). *Dare to lead: Brave work, tough conversations, whole hearts*. New York: Random House.

Claessens, B., van Eerde, W., Rutte, C., & Roe, R. (2007). A review of the time management literature. *Time Management Literature, 36*(2), 255–270.

Coggins, C. (2008). The post-boomer teacher crunch. *Education Week, 27*(32), 26–27.

Collins, J. (2009). *How the mighty fall*. New York: Harper Collins.

Covey, S. (1996). *First things first*. New York: Simon & Schuster.

DialogueWorks (2020). *Do you empower your people? 10 strategies for empowering others*. Retrieved online from www.dialogueworks.

com/blog/do-you-empower-your-people-10-strategies-for-empowering-others

Dinkmeyer, D., & Losoncy, L. (Eds.). (1980). *The encouragement book*. New York: Simon and Schuster.

DuFour, Ri, DuFour, Re, Eaker, R. & Many, T. (2006). *Learning by doing: A handbook for professional learning communities at work*. Bloomington, IN: Solution Tree.

Dweck, C. (2013). *Mindset: The new psychology of success*. New York: Ballantine Books.

Esteve, M., & Schuster, C. (2019). *Motivating public employees*. Cambridge: Cambridge University Press.

Fowler, S. (2017). *Why motivating people doesn't work ... and what does*. San Francisco: Berrett-Koehler Publishers, Inc.

Fox, M. (2021). *Teacher retirements were up in 2020, and mor are expected in 2021*. Retrieved online from www.wpr.org/teacher-retirements-were-2020-and-more-are-expected-2

Fullan, M. (2015). *The new meaning of educational change*. New York: Routledge.

Fuscaldo, D. (2021). *Managing Gen Z in the workplace*. Retrieved online from www.businessnewsdaily.com/15873-managing-gen-z.html

Gallo, A. (2016). How to manage a toxic employee. *Harvard Business Review*. Retrieved online from https://hbr.org/2016/10/how-to-manage-a-toxic-employee

Garmston, R., & Wellman, B. (2013). *The adaptive school: A sourcebook for developing collaborative groups* (2nd ed.). Norwood, MA: Christopher-Gordon.

Goldberg, E. (2021). *As pandemic upends teacher, fewer students want to pursue it*. Retrieved online from www.nytimes.com/2021/03/27/us/covid-school-teaching.html

Gomez, K., Mawhinney, T., & Betts, K. (2020). *Understanding generation Z in the workplace*. Retrieved online from https://www2.deloitte.com/us/en/pages/consumer-business/articles/understanding-generation-z-in-the-workplace.html

Gomez, K., Mawhinney, T., & Betts, K. (2022). *Welcome to generation Z*. Retrieved online from https://www2.deloitte.com/content/dam/Deloitte/us/Documents/consumer-business/welcome-to-gen-z.pdf

Graham, J. (2002). *Balancing work and family*. University of Maine. Retrieved from http://umaine.edu/publications/4186e/

Hirsch, S., & Killion, J. (2007). *The learning educator: A new era of professional learning*. Oxford, OH: Learning Forward.

Hoy, W., & Tarter, C. (2008). *Administrators solving the problems of practice: Decision-making concepts, cases and consequences* (3rd ed.). Boston: Pearson Education.

Johnson, B. (2019). *Putting teachers first: How to inspire, motivate, and connect with your staff*. New York: Routledge.

Kamenetz, A. (2022). *More than half of teachers are looking for the exits*. Retrieved online from www.npr.org/2022/02/01/1076943883/teachers-quitting-burnout

Kouzes, J., & Posner, B. (2011). *Credibility: How leaders gain and lose it, why people demand it*. San Francisco: Jossey-Bass.

Leong, J., & Raphael, J. (2019). *Lesson study participant guide*. Education Northwest. Retrieved from https://educationnorthwest.org/sites/default/files/lesson-study-participant-guide.pdf

Marshall, K. (2008). The big rocks: Priority management for principals. *Principal Leadership, 8*(7), 16–22.

Maslow, A. (1968). *Toward a psychology of being*. New York: Van Nostrand.

McGregor, J. (2020). *Remote work really does mean longer days – and more meetings*. Washington Post. Retrieved online from www.washingtonpost.com/business/2020/08/04/remote-work-longer-days/

Miller, H. (2022). 10 ways of building trust as a leader. *Leaders.com*. Retrieved July 20, 2022, from https://leaders.com/articles/company-culture/building-trust/

Mind Tools (2023). *Authenticity*. Retrieved online from https://mindtools.com/ay30irc/authenticity

Morgenstern, J. (2005). *Never check email in the morning and other unexpected strategies for making your work life work*. Toronto: Fireside Publishing.

Nelson, C., & Dunsmore, K. (2018). *A leader's guide to building instructional capacity*. Retrieved online from www.norc.org/PDFs/LOCI/District%20Capacity%20White%20Paper_2018.pdf

Newton, S. (2017). Five essentials for building leadership capacity. *Principal Leadership*, 18(4). Retrieved online from www.nassp.org/publication/principal-leadership/volume-18-2017-2018/principal-leadership-december-2017/five-essentials-for-building-teacher-leadership-capacity/

Peterson, K. D., & Deal, T. E. (2009). *The shaping school culture fieldbook* (2nd ed.). San Francisco, CA: Jossey-Bass.

Pink, D. (2009). *Drive: The surprising truth about what motivates us*. New York: Penguin Books.

Porath, C. (2016). *Mastering civility: A manifesto for the workplace*. New York: Grand Central Publishing.

Rogers, S. (2021). *From boomers to Zoomers, here are the characteristics of the different generations at work*. Retrieved online from www.getapp.com/resources/characteristics-of-different-generations-in-the-workplace/

Shapiro, J., & Stefkovich, J. (2021). *Ethical leadership and decision making in education: Applying theoretical perspectives to complex dilemmas* (5th ed.). New York: Routledge.

Uscher, J. (2011). *5 tips for better work-life balance*. WebMD. Retrieved from www.webmd.com/women/features/balance-life

Whitaker, K. (1996). Exploring causes of principal burnout. *Journal of Educational Administration, 34*(1), 60–71.

Williamson, R. (2009). *Scheduling to improve student learning*. Westerville, OH: National Middle School Association.

Williamson, R., & Blackburn, B. (2016). *The principalship from A to Z* (2nd ed.). New York: Routledge.

Williamson, R., & Blackburn, B. (2019). *Seven strategies for improving your school*. New York: Routledge.

Williamson, R., & Blackburn, B. (2020). *7 strategies for improving your school*. New York: Routledge Eye on Education.

Williamson, R., & Blackburn, B. (2021a). *10 actions help navigate challenge and dissent*. MilldeWeb. Retrieved online from www.middleweb.com/45843/10-strategies-to-navigate-challenge-and-dissent/

Williamson, R., & Blackburn, B. (2021b). *Leadership for remote learning: Strategies for success*. New York: Routledge Eye on Education.

Williamson, R., & Blackburn, B. (2021c). *Leadership for remote learning: Strategies for success*. New York: Routledge.

Williamson, R., & Johnson, J. H. (2012). *The school leader's guide to social media*. New York: Routledge Eye on Education.

Zak, P. (2019). How our brains decide when to trust. *Harvard Business Review*. Retrieved July 20, 2022, from https://hbr.org/2019/07/how-our-brains-decide-when-to-trust

Zenger, J., & Folkman, J. (2019). The 3 elements of trust. *Harvard Business Review*. Retrieved July 20, 2022, from https://hbr.org/2019/02/the-3-elements-of-trust

For Product Safety Concerns and Information please contact our EU
representative GPSR@taylorandfrancis.com
Taylor & Francis Verlag GmbH, Kaufingerstraße 24, 80331 München, Germany

www.ingramcontent.com/pod-product-compliance
Lightning Source LLC
Chambersburg PA
CBHW050555300426
44112CB00013B/1921